THE PRACTICES OF ANCIENT EGYPTIAN RITUAL AND MAGIC

Published by Avalonia

BM Avalonia
London
WC1N 3XX
England, UK

www.avaloniabooks.co.uk

First Edition January 2006
Copyright © David Rankine & Avalonia

Book Design by Avalonia
Illustrations by Brian Andrews © 2005
Cover Design by Satori © 2005

ISBN 1-905297-07-6

HEKA

THE PRACTICES OF ANCIENT EGYPTIAN RITUAL AND MAGIC

David Rankine

Acknowledgements

My love of Egyptian culture and magic has grown over a very long period of time. However certain authors have particularly inspired me with their work and scholarship. For this reason I would particularly like to thank Geraldine Pinch, whose work more than any other has continued to inspire me through the years.

I would also like to thank Geraldine Beskin and Helen Hodge for their continued encouragement and support during the writing of this book.

More than anyone else, this work is dedicated to Sorita D'Este, without whose inspiration, support and assistance, it would not have been possible.

Table of Contents

Table of Figures

Introduction

The religious and magical practices of the ancient Egyptians have had a profound and lasting effect on the world. Egypt has been described as the *"mother of magicians"*.[1] To appreciate the Egyptian view of magic, we need to accept that to the Egyptians magic was not considered strange or eccentric, but was a part of daily life, to which everyone resorted. Magic blended seamlessly with religion and medicine, being seen as part of a holistic worldview.

This universality of magic seems strange to us today, in a world where magic has been compartmentalised and marginalized to the fringes of society. However magic was as much a part of daily life as food or drink, and had no stigma attached to it. Magic was a fact of life, and part of the cycle of eternity that ensured order in human existence. Magic was seen as a positive and indeed vitally necessary part of existence, not a threatening or unnatural negative force.

The influence of Egyptian magic has persisted through to the present day, and is one of the dominant threads in the Western Mystery Tradition. However despite its popularity, people have tended to draw from the funerary texts, like the *Pyramid Texts* and *Coffin Texts*, and the *Book of the Dead*, for sources to incorporate into their magic. This is a fundamentally flawed approach, as the funerary texts dealt specifically with the journey of the soul after death through the underworld.

The magic used in daily life, known as heka, bore little resemblance to this funerary magic. Unfortunately little work has been done to explore the practices of the magicians and priests practising heka. The main exceptions to this are Geraldine Pinch's excellent academic work *Magic in Ancient Egypt* and Robert Kreich Ritner's *Mechanics of Ancient Egyptian Magical Practice*, which focuses largely on the priestly and pharaonic practise of heka for the benefit and protection of society. In this volume I am seeking to redress this balance, looking at what is known of the practices and symbolism used by practitioners of heka.

A quick perusal of the material covered will soon demonstrate that Egypt deserved its title as *mother of magicians*, for within the ancient

---

[1] Clement of Alexandria.

Egyptian practices will be found the forerunners of most techniques used today by practising occultists. From the techniques used for creation of sacred space to the purification and preparation required to practice magic, the ancient Egyptians laid lasting foundations for the development of the subsequent magical traditions, as visible in current practice as the Pyramids are in the Egyptian landscape!

In presenting this material I have endeavoured to place it within the context of the ancient Egyptian worldview as far as I am able, albeit limited by the knowledge we have thousands of years later. The glory of ancient Egypt spanned a period of around three thousand years, so inevitably during this time practices evolved or fell into disuse, and foreign influences crept in. Obviously we are not in ancient Egypt any more, and the level to which you may choose to recreate the practices of heka within your own magic is your decision.

I have included as much detail as possible about the various materials used by the ancient Egyptians, including food, crystals, metals, woods, incense materials, etc, so that you may work with the same materials if you wish to. Remember that the Egyptian magicians were rigorous in maintaining the discipline of good hygiene and timing!

You may be puzzled at the absence of information on hieroglyphics in this book. However as this volume is focused on techniques and information, I leave it to the reader to pursue this topic in one of the already extant works that cover the field admirably, such as Sir Alan Gardiner's *Egyptian Grammar* or James Allen's *Middle Egyptian*.

I hope you enjoy finding out more about heka, and may you always uphold Maat in all that you do.

David Rankine
London
December 2005

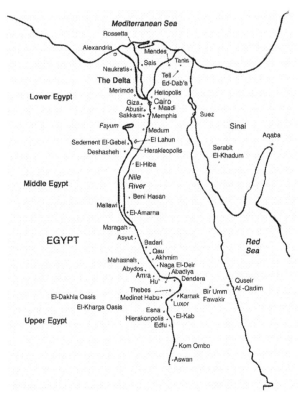

Figure 1 : Map of Egypt

PART I

ANCIENT PERSPECTIVES

1. What is Heka?

The word heka can mean several things, each contributing to our understanding of the complexities of ancient Egyptian magic. The function of heka is described in the *Instruction for Merikara*, the Middle Kingdom teaching of the Pharaoh Amenemhet I (c. 2000 BCE):

> *"He [Re] gave them [mankind] the heka as a weapon in order to ward off the effect of dangerous events."* [2]

Heka was seen as a gift from the sun god Re to mankind (his offspring), a manifestation of his creative energy as an embodiment of his Ba (his soul). It empowered man to create using words and actions, mirroring the sun god's creation of the universe. Heka can be seen as the creative force or life-giving energy connecting the objects, links and symbols of life with the universe, like a subtle tapestry of energy, which the magician must learn to read if s/he is to effectively work magic.

Heka is also the inherent magical energy (mana or *personal power*) found within living beings. Different creatures were perceived as possessing different amounts of heka. The gods had the most heka. The pharaoh (as a channel for the divine energy) also had a lot of heka, as did people who were considered unusual, such as dwarfs and people with birth defects. Red hair was considered a sign of having much heka, due to the magical associations with that colour. And of course the other class of being with a lot of heka was the dead, hence the use of spells calling on the dead to assist with performing rites.

Today the practice of heka is open to anyone who wishes to pursue it. Although we do not have the worldview of the ancient Egyptians and much of their material has been lost, we do have some major advantages that make heka more accessible.

For a start literacy and numeracy are the norm, rather than being restricted to the rich and priestly castes, as was the case in Egypt. Technology has made the power of the written and spoken words, so vital to Egyptian magic, available to all of us. For this reason you do not need to have a university education or have studied Egyptology or classics to appreciate Egyptian magic. Freedom of information has brought truth to the statement that *magic is for all,* or rather meant that is accessible to all who have the desire and dedication to pursue a magical life.

---

[2] *The Mecanics of Ancient Egyptian Magical Practice*, R.K. Ritner, 1993.

As well as being the term for magic, Heka was a god, indeed he was the god of magic. Or perhaps it would be more correct to say he was magic, being the divine personification of magic. He is sometimes shown in images as appearing among the crew of the solar barque. He was depicted as a bearded man wearing a lion nemes headdress.

Another definition of heka is given in funerary spell 261 of the *Coffin Texts*, from a Middle Kingdom sarcophagus. The spell is entitled *"To become the god Heka"*, and reads:

> *"I am he whom the Lord of all [3] made before duality had yet come into being ... the son of him who gave birth to the universe ... I am the protection of that which the Lord of all has ordained ... I am he who gave life to the Ennead of the gods ... come to take my position that I may receive my dignity. Because to me belonged the universe before you gods had come into being. You have come afterwards because I am Heka."* [4]

The hieroglyph used from 1000 BCE to write his name was interchangeable with the concepts of *god* and *power*. Visually the hieroglyph depicted the hindquarters of a lion, and may well be linked with his attribution as one of the sons of the lion-headed goddess Sekhmet. In this form he was shown as a young child with a solar disk on his head.

With Sekhmet's son Nefertem (purity) being considered to be an avatar of the Sun God Re, it is possible that Heka may also have been seen in this light. This presents a line of apostolic succession of power, from Re to his daughter Sekhmet, and hence to her sons Heka and Nefertem, who also embody the qualities of Re between them.

One of the titles of the god Heka was The one who consecrates imagery, referring to the ability of the god to empower creative thoughts and actions and translate them into their physical equivalents in the physical world. So Heka was also perceived as the animating and manifesting force of every ritual act. In this context heka is thus both intent and action: the cause, the act and the effect.

From the point of view of *Sau* (the magical use of amulets), this title is extremely suggestive, as any amulet or talisman is ultimately an image that is given form and then consecrated with the power of Heka. So not only is Heka the god who consecrates the image, but it is his power that is relied upon to create the image.

---

[3] i.e. Re, the Sun God and Progenitor of the Gods.
[4] *The Ancient Egyptian Coffin Texts*, R.O. Faulkner, 1973.

Figure 2 : The God Heka

Another title of the god Heka was Lord of Ka's, referring to the soul. This is a significant title, as all mankind and even the gods have ka's. In the Middle to Late Kingdom Heka becomes seen as the ka of Re, with Re declaring, *"Heka is my ka."* From this perspective Heka can be seen as being as significant as Maat as part of the underlying force and flow behind the whole of the cosmos.

Coffin Text spell 648 stresses not only the role of Heka as Lord of Ka's, but also as the power the gods used, and the inherent magic of the word:

> *"His powers put fear into the gods who came into being after him, his myriad of spirits is within his mouth. It was Heka who came into being of himself, at seeing whom the gods rejoiced, and through the sweet savour of whom the gods live, who created the mountains and knit the firmament together."* [5]

In conjunction with Sia (Perception) and Hu (Creative logos), Heka was involved in the creation of the first time and the separation of heaven and earth. This is one of the reasons why these deities are shown in the solar barque of Re, as they are all part of the process of first creation, which the magician returns to by creating a sacred space and performing magic (heka).

This is also why he is *"Heka who opens his two eyes that the two lands might see"*, for he is the agent of Re, whose perception (Sia) and utterance (Hu) empowered by magic (Heka) ensures the continuances of the cycle of daily creation.

Heka is also referred to as the Elder Magician, emphasising his primal nature as the first child of Atum-Re, and distinguishing him from younger deities of magic who draw ultimately on his power, like Isis.

As has already been mentioned, Re declares that Heka is his ba, and this is stated unequivocally in *The Book of the Heavenly Cow*, where Re declares:

> *"I am the one who made heaven and who established it in order to places the ba's of the gods within it. I shall be with them for eternity which time begets. My ba is Heka. It is older than it [time] ... the ba of Re is in Heka throughout the entire land."* [6]

The association between Heka and Maat is indicated in one of the *Vienna Papyri*, where Heka is described as "Controller of the House of Natural Law". Natural law is the function of Maat, so this implies the function of magic as part of the normal functioning of the universe, within the balance of Maat.

---

[5] *The Ancient Egyptian Coffin Texts*, R.O. Faulkner, 1973.
[6] *Ancient Egyptian Magical Texts*, J.F. Borghouts, 1978.

The title *Wer-Hekau*, meaning *Mighty of Magic*, is derived from heka. This title was used by several of the major deities, all of whom were particularly linked with magical powers, specifically Anubis, Isis and Thoth.

Originally Weret-Hekau (the Great of Magic) was a cobra goddess, whose form may have survived into serpent wands, but she was assimilated into other deities like Isis at a very early stage. She also had a lioness form, thus possessing the qualities of the two most common powerful creatures amongst the deities.

Heka needs to be distinguished from other forms of magic to appreciate its usage in ancient Egypt. As well as heka there was *akhu*, the spells or enchantments practised by the dead; and *sau*, which was amuletic magic.

It should be stressed that heka was largely used as a preventative form of magic, a sort of ancient crisis management, to help deal with events like animal attacks, infectious diseases, disasters, and of course the perils of childbirth. Anti-social magic (i.e. cursing) did not really form a part of heka until the Roman influence in the latter days of ancient Egypt. As such heka is ideal for anyone wishing to develop themselves through pursuing a positive magical and spiritual path.

The one example of heka being used as *black magic* comes from the 19th Dynasty. The Harim Conspiracy involved several functionaries using written magical spells, wax figurines and potions to attempt to kill Ramesses III. The conspirators of this failed attempt at regicide received the death sentence and also the ultimate punishment given to traitors and enemies of the state. All traces of their names were removed from existence, as if they had never existed, so that their being was annihilated.

The major instance of heka being used in a manner that would be seen today as black magic was the practice of cursing against enemies of the state by the Pharaoh, such as enemy armies. Details of such techniques are recorded in the so-called *Execration Texts*, which are not covered in the current volume as they are not relevant to the personal practice of Heka. This however was not seen as cursing, as it was an effort to protect the sovereignty of Egypt. In such instances sympathetic magic on a grand scale might be resorted to, with models representing enemy ships or troops being ritually destroyed.

If somebody was having problems, with illness or bad luck, this was often viewed as the actions of beings with heka. It could be an angry ghost, a sorceror, or an angry deity that the individual had offended. To this end the individual was seen as the victim of circumstances, and there was no guilt associated with seeking a practitioner of heka to help fight off the negative influences being experienced. By restoring the correct balance problems were resolved, again demonstrating the nature of heka as being the natural and correct flow of energy towards harmony within the universe.

It has been suggested that there was a separate class of magicians operating on the fringes of society performing heka for the masses, but evidence now indicates that the practitioners of heka were usually none other than priests, acting as magicians and earning an income outside of their temple duties. Priests served one month in four in the temple and spent the other three months with their families, were they were not bound by all the same taboos and strictures as when serving the gods in the temple. During this time in the community they were thus available to assist members of the community who might need their aid.

The word heka continued to be used through until Roman times. After this it was succeeded by the Coptic word *hik* (xik), which was equated to the Greek word *mageia* (and hence magic).

2. Worldview

The ancient Egyptian worldview was very different from our own. To keep perspective of the practices and changes that occurred, it must be remembered that the dynastic history of ancient Egypt spanned over 3,000 years of history. A brief chronology is provided below to give a chronological context to the material within this book.

Period	Timescale
Predynastic	5500-3200 BCE
Protodynastic	3200-3100 BCE
Early Dynastic Period, Dynasties 1-2	3100-2686 BCE
Old Kingdom, Dynasties 3-6	2686-2181 BCE
First Intermediate Period, Dynasties 7-10	2181-2055 BCE
Middle Kingdom, Dynasties 11-13	2055-1650 BCE
Second Intermediate Period, Dynasties 14-17	1650-1550 BCE
New Kingdom, Dynasties 18-20	1550-1069 BCE
Third Intermediate Period, Dynasties 21-24	1069-747 BCE
Late Period, Dynasties 25-30	747-332 BCE
Macedonian Dynasty	332-310 BCE
Ptolemaic Dynasty	305-30 BCE
Roman Period	30 BCE – 395 CE

Revising your Worldview

The Egyptians saw the universe as being made of four worlds – the everyday world we live in, the underworld, the sky and the heavens. If we consider the story of Geb and Nuit being separated by Shu, who holds Nuit away from Geb, we can see this in more perspective.

Re was said to be jealous of the closeness of Nuit (the heavens) with her brother and lover Geb (the earth). So Re ordered Shu (the air) to separate the lovers. Subsequently in response to the pregnant Nuit's pleas, Thoth played draughts with the moon and won five extra days. On each of these extra days, Nuit bore a child. These were Osiris, Horus the Elder, Set, Isis and Nephthys.

By these actions two major aspects of the Egyptian worldview are explained. The first is the expansion of the year from 360 days (the perfect circle of 360°) formed by the twelve 30 day months, to the 365-day year we have become familiar with by the addition of the Epagomenal days.

The second is the structure of the cosmos. For Shu is the air, or sky, through which Re journeys each day. Above the sky are the heavens, the body of Nuit, containing all the stars. Below the sky is the earth, the body of Geb. And of course below the earth is the underworld, through which Re travels every night.

Within the body of Nuit were the stars and other planets. These were seen as celestial manifestations of the gods, with certain planets and stars being particularly associated with specific deities.

The most significant star was Sirius, which had its own goddess Sothis (Sopdet), who rose in the heavens to signal the vital inundation of the Nile. The god Sah was the husband of Sothis, and he represented Orion. These two stars were subsequently attributed to Isis and Osiris. The Great Bear was associated with Set and Regulus with Re.

Of the planets, Venus, Mars, Jupiter and Saturn were all associated with aspects of Horus. It seems likely that the fiery Mercury was associated with Set. The Moon of course was associated with the moon god Khonsu and with Thoth.

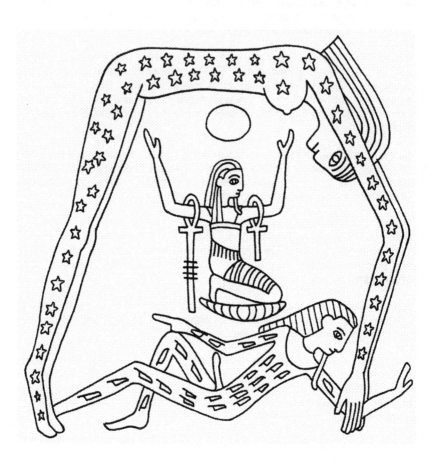

Figure 3 : Nuit & Geb

The Sacred Landscape

Sacred geometry was another key element of the Egyptian worldview. The construction of the pyramids and temples reflected the perception of the cosmos. Large pylon gateways represented the mountains of the eastern horizon where the Sun God rose, and sacred lakes representing the primeval waters of chaos. By bathing in these waters and then stepping onto the land, a priest was replicating the acts of the gods, rising from the primeval waters.

This brings us to a very important consideration, which is how the landscape shapes the perceptions of those who live within it. Central to the Egyptian worldview was the desert that surrounded them, and the Nile as the focus of life, through its fertile waters, and the black Nile mud that helped the crops grow. The Nile also enabled the rapid transport of foodstuffs and materials, and ensured the development of the towns and cities along it as centres of trade.

The North-South axis of the Nile served as the focus for the society and culture of Egypt. This is reflected by the importance attached to the Nile in religion, art and trade. The East-West axis of the Sun God's journey provided the other focus, bringing the order and structure of religion and time into daily life.

Away from the Nile the desert landscape is bleak and fierce, and the hostility of this landscape is also reflected in the deities whose nature embodied chaos or the ferocity of the desert sun. The 90% or so of Egypt that was desert was known as the "Red land" in contrast to the "Black land" of the Nile and its environs. At the boundaries and in the bleak lands supernatural creatures and enemies roamed, making the security and stability of Egypt of prime importance to its inhabitants.

At the beginning of the Dynasties the Egyptians had no idea of the size of the world. To them the world extended from Greece and Turkey in the north, to Ethiopia in the South, from Iraq in the east to Libya in the west. Obviously these are modern countries and not the names the Egyptians were familiar with, but it shows how little of the globe the Egyptians were aware of. To the Egyptians they were at the centre of the created world, which was a flat disk.

The underside of the disk was the *Duat* or underworld, which largely reflected the upper surface of the earth. As the disk was surrounded by water, the Egyptians perceived the circumference of the disk as being marshes.

At the edge of the earth was the *Akhet*, the region which the sun passed through to emerge from and descend into the night sky. This was why the sun did not emerge suddenly in the morning or instantly disappear at night, but went through a process of fading at sunset and appearing gradually in the morning.

Beyond foreign countries were the primeval waters of Nun, the original chaos, which they also saw as the ultimate source of the Nile. The waters of Nun also rose above and below the disk, encompassing it in a great bubble of water, the surface of which was Nuit, the sky. Nuit formed the boundary between the atmosphere (Shu) and the waters of Nun.

Whilst today we view the world with a focus to the north as being upwards, for the Egyptians south was the upward direction, as South-North was the directional flow of the Nile. Southern Egypt was known as Upper Egypt, and Northern Egypt as Lower Egypt.

The Heart and the Mouth

Today we know a lot about the workings of the brain and the cognitive process, but to the Egyptians the heart was the centre of intelligence. This is why it is the heart that is weighed against the feather of truth in the scales of judgement in the underworld.

In the Memphite theology, Ptah creates the universe from the *"thoughts of his heart and the words of his mouth"*. Another myth gives Thoth as the creator of the universe by uttering the first word. Both these myths emphasise the power of words to create, a key factor in understanding the ancient Egyptian worldview.

The mouth as uttering the words had great power, as did saliva, being formed in the mouth. One myth has the great chaos serpent Apophis being formed from saliva from the goddess Neith, and the myth of Isis stealing Re's true name involves her using some of his saliva to form a serpent that poisons him, which only she can cure.

Wisdom Texts

Part of the Egyptian worldview was in the personal ethics that people learned. Because a person's earthly actions would have a bearing on their status in the underworld, and indeed if their soul even survived to get there, good behaviour was strongly emphasised.

In the Middle Kingdom texts known as Instructions in Wisdom (the so-called *Wisdom Texts*) became popular, and were taught to children. These texts were said to have been authorized by the gods, and emphasised balance and order (Maat), good conduct and manners, moderation and righteousness. Through these instructions people learned how to be positive members of the community, how to behave towards the gods and what was expected of them in different circumstances. Those who did live their lives according to Maat were known as still, silent or knowledgeable men, those who did not were called fools.

The Role of the Pharaoh

The following quote illustrates much of the Egyptian worldview, describing the role of the king as intermediary between his people and the gods.

"Re has placed the king in the land of the living, forever and ever, judging humankind and satisfying the gods, realising Maat and destroying Isfet.
He (the king) gives offerings to the gods and mortuary offerings to the deceased." [7]

The word *isfet* means lack, and refers to concepts of disorder, like sickness, injustice, falsehood, starvation, violence, war, etc. By upholding Maat, the natural order is preserved. The importance of making offerings to the gods and the ancestors is also stressed.

Maat

Although different gods were worshipped in different parts of Egypt, and rose and fell in significance, the children of Re were of central importance to the daily cycle of life. Amongst the gods present in the solar barque with Re were various deities he was said to have fathered in one manner or another.

Amongst these were Heka, Hu and Sia, providing the magical energies and their means of manifestation. Also present was Maat, said to be his daughter, who was central to the whole Egyptian worldview. To indicate why this is so, I shall consider her nature and roles in more detail.

Maat embodied the concepts of truth, justice and cosmic order. She is mentioned in the Pyramid Texts as standing behind Re, implying that she is the source of his power. In this context she is described as giving delight to Re and giving *"life to his nostrils"* (note the importance of breath again). As time passed she became seen as the daughter of Re, and also as the wife of Thoth, God of Magic, who put the laws of Maat into writing. Maat was also sometimes partnered (though not as wife) with Heka.

---

[7] Agyptische Hymen und Gebete, J Assmann, no 20, lines 31-37

Figure 4 : The Goddess Maat

Maat was usually depicted as a beautiful young woman with wings and her symbol of the white ostrich feather on her head. The feather implies air and the breath of life, implicit in terms found in ancient Egyptian texts like *breathing in Maat.*

The term upholding Maat was sometimes used to describe the practice of heka. Maat is central to the practice of Egyptian magic and religion, and in some respects can be seen as the most important deity of the whole pantheon.

Maat had several major roles in the continued well-being of Gods and men. One of her symbols was the hieroglyph of the plinth on which statues stood, implying the supremacy of Maat, representing the order that even the gods strive to perceive. This may be seen through Maat shrines usually being present in the temples of other gods rather than being distinct, and also statements like "the gods live on Maat.

The most significant role of the Pharaoh was to uphold Maat, and the success of his reign would be measured by how well he did this. Many of the Pharaohs took the title "beloved of Maat" to emphasise their position. One of the most important ceremonies performed by the Pharaoh was the presentation of Maat, where he would make a ritual presentation of a Maat statue in the Temple of the Gods, saying *"I give you Maat with my left hand, my right hand protecting her".* The presentation was most often made to creator gods, like Amun, Re and Ptah.

As the goddess of justice Maat was the patron of judges, they wore small gold pendants of her as a sign of their authority. Reference is made to magicians painted depictions of Maat as a feather onto their tongues with magical ink to demonstrate they spoke only words of truth when performing their spells.

In her role of goddess of the balance in the underworld, Maat was the central figure of this rite of passage. Her feather of truth was weighed on the scales against the heart, and she also presided over the weighing with Osiris in his role as Lord of the Underworld. The weighing took place in the Hall of Two Truths, and Maat was often depicted in twin form here. The gods who acted as the judges of the divine tribunal of the soul were called the *Council of Maat.*

The soul of the deceased had to recite the Negative Confessions, forty-two statements of good conduct that were seen as guidelines to living a balanced life, a life of Maat. If the heart of the deceased then balanced against the feather, the deceased was judged to be *"true of heart and voice"* and would live with the gods. If not they were fed to Ammut, the devourer of souls, and annihilated.

A clear parallel can be seen between the forty-two pylons or portals to be passed through on the journey to the Hall of Two Truths, the forty-two judges of the Divine Tribunal and the corresponding number of negative confessions that had to be made. Due to her role in the underworld, the term "joining Maat" came to be used as a euphemism for dying.

Maat had a variety of titles, which emphasise her roles in the ancient Egyptian cosmology.

These epithets include:

- Directress of the Underworld.
- Justice.
- Lady of the Hall of Judgment.
- Lady of the Heavens Queen of Earth.
- Law.
- Maat the Beautiful.
- Perfect Measure.
- Right Order.
- Sustainer of the Sun.
- The Changeless.
- The Good Gift.
- The Undeviating.
- That which Is True.
- Tracer of the Course of the Sun.
- Truth.
- Twofold Truth.
- The Measure of the Heart.

Interacting with the Gods

The way in which the Egyptians interacted with their gods is also very different to the way modern pagans do today. If it did not seem like a deity was giving the required aid, Egyptians would plead with and command them to carry out tasks for them. The gods, although immortal, were seen as being subject to the laws of Maat like everything else, and could ultimately be killed, as Osiris was.

As a result the Egyptians would threaten their gods, with threats such as smashing their statues, burning down temples and killing their sacred animals if they did not feel they were doing enough to help them.

This is illustrated in a love spell on a 20th Dynasty pottery fragment:

*"If you do not make her come after me,
Then I will set fire to Busiris and burn up Osiris"* [8]

Many of the spells and rituals rely on the magician assimilating the deity into himself, effectively becoming the deity, and so gaining the powers associated with that deity. By becoming the deity a magician greatly increased his level of heka, ensuring the effectiveness of the magic he would perform. This was possible through the immanence of the gods. Apart from Amun, the hidden creative force, almost all the gods existed tangibly. Thus Geb was the earth beneath people's feet, Shu was the air they breathed and the winds that blew around them, Sekhmet was the ferocity of the midday sun and the mother lion, etc.

In a modern context we can see this practice as gaining the positive qualities of the deity. Images and statues of the gods were essential, and are a must for a modern practitioner of heka. These images act as a gateway for the power of the gods, enabling it to be transmitted to you as the agent of change.

From the Early Kingdom magicians were also known as prophets of Heka, an interesting title when considering later texts like the Greco-Egyptian Headless One9, where the magician states "I am thy prophet".

Ancestor Worship and the Afterlife

Another important consideration was that the dead did not become disempowered forgotten figures. The dead were believed to be contactable, and could be petitioned for their aid, as they possessed more heka than the living. This is why Egyptians used *letters to the Dead* to petition the aid of the dead in righting injustices that had been perpetrated on them.

Ancestor worship as a manifestation of this reverence for and contact with the dead was widespread. Food that was initially offered to the gods in the daily ceremonies would then be ritually removed and offered to the ancestors to give them sustenance as well, before again being ritually removed and eaten by the priests.

We should also note that the ancient Egyptians did not view demons as negative figures either. They were not seen as the deceptive and malefic forces that modern magic often portrays them as, or as aspects of the psyche of the magician. Demons were known to be fearsome inhabitants of the underworld, who could be communicated with and appealed to for assistance without any feeling of spiritual danger.

---

[8] *Ancient Egyptian Magic*, Bob Brier, 1980.
[9] Popularly known today as *The Bornless Ritual*.

The gods lived in the Fields of Reeds (also called the Field of Offerings and the Beautiful West). The Fields of Reeds were an idealized version of Egypt itself, with the same geography, but more fertile. This overlaying of the physical and divine realms meant there was a sense of familiarity with the afterlife to come.

It also meant that practitioners of heka, when stepping back to the original creation within their sacred space, could call on the gods to help create change that would manifest from the divine realm through to the physical. This concept of the overlaying of a more ethereal idealised version of the landscape may also be the origin of the idea of the lower astral plane being a concurrent reproduction of the physical plane.

The different parts of the Soul

The ancient Egyptians believed in the plurality of the soul, with each part representing different qualities or aspects of the individual. This is significant as different gods were sometimes considered to represent aspects of the souls of other deities. These parts were:

- Ab – the heart, centre of moral awareness and good and evil. The Ab lived with the gods if it passes judgement, balancing Maat's feather of Truth.
- Akhu – meaning effective one, the radiant immortal part of the person, created by the uniting of Ba and Ka and residing in the Sahu.
- Ba – can be translated as impression, and depicted as a human-headed bird, this part of the soul represented the personality of the person.
- Ka – the life-force.
- Khabait – the shadow, that could partake of funerary offerings for sustenance, and leave the tomb.
- Ren – the true name of a person, describing their essence.
- Sahu – the vessel of the spiritual body.
- Sekhem – the ethereal personification of the life force of the person.

In the context of the soul's nature, it should be emphasised, that as with many other of the early religions drawn upon as sources for modern paganism (such as ancient Greece, Rome, Norse, etc), the ancient Egyptian religion had no doctrine of reincarnation. Instead they believed that a person had only one life in a physical body.

3. The Deities

The family of Egyptian gods is extremely complex, and made of several diverse parts. Over the centuries some of the relationships were changed, as the cults of different deities gained power. Obviously there are many Egyptian deities, and I am giving an overview here of the major deities and the qualities they display. This then enables you to determine which deity it is most relevant to work with for the results you are striving for. To cover the gods in more detail would require many books, and there are several excellent books on the Egyptian gods available.

Egyptian deity names were often written in red to show the power of the deity, red being associated with power and danger to the ancient Egyptians. This practice continued into the medieval Grimoires, with the names of god and angels usually being written in red. The use of colour was highly significant to the Egyptians, and should be to you too.

As the Egyptians believed words had an inherent power, the names of gods were believed to have especially strong power. This is why deities were often referred to by titles, e.g. Thoth as Wer-hekau or Mighty one of Magic. With time the cults of different deities rose and fell, and other deities took control of and assimilated titles which once belonged to other gods. A good examples to illustrate this is that of Khenti-Amenti (whose name means Foremost of the Westerners), a wolf-headed death god, who was assimilated into the worship and cult of Anubis. Later, as the worship of Osiris became more powerful and prominent, this title became ascribed to him.

Many of the names of the deities represented the forces they embodied, like Nuit, Geb, Tefnut and Maat. Other names describe roles or qualities associated with the deity, as in the case of deities like Horus, Set and Thoth. The names of gods usually ended with the generic determinative for god, and goddesses with the determinative for woman. There were exceptions to this, which all tend to be for the earliest gods, who often have their own unique special determinative, such as Anubis, Atum, Maat, Osiris and Set.

Another consideration with the gods was that their eye colours were considered to give indications to their nature. Thus we find it recorded that Horus had lapis lazuli coloured eyes, Re had electrum (silver and gold) coloured eyes, Atum had green eyes, and predatory and feline gods like Set and Sekhmet had red eyes. The gods are usually described as being around 8 cubits tall, i.e. around 4.5m. Obviously this is the height you would use in visualisations of the deities for meditations, pathworkings, etc.

Some strands of modern magic do not attach much significance to the gods, but in heka the gods are paramount. It is impossible to practice Egyptian magic without incorporating the symbols and worship of the gods, as the distinction between magic and religion did not exist for the ancient Egyptians. For this reason I have included details about the appropriate symbols and concepts associated with the deities, so they can be incorporated in magical work to help develop your relationship with the deities.

Major Triads

These triads both fit into the family of gods, but not into the direct line of descent seen in the main family tree (apart from Sekhmet). Here we can see the major creator gods of Amun (from the Ogdoad) and Ptah being fitted into the cosmology to make it still workable as a whole.

Amun + Mut = Khonsu

Ptah + Sekhmet = Nefertem

The Ogdoad

The Ogdoad of Hermopolis was identified as four frog-headed gods and four serpent-headed goddesses who were their consorts, and who represented the sum of existence before creation. Of these Amun developed to become the dominant and evolving god, with Mut supplanting Amaunet as his partner.

God	Goddess	Representing
Nun	Naunet	Water
Heh	Hauhet	Infinity
Kek	Kauket	Darkness
Amun	Amaunet	Hiddenness / Wind

The Ennead

The Great Ennead was that of Heliopolis, which comprised of the line of descent from Atum through to his great-grandchildren (i.e. Osiris and Set, Isis and Nephthys). It comprised of Shu and Tefnut, their children Geb and Nuit, and their children Osiris, Isis, Set, Nephthys and Horus the Elder.

Amun

Amun translates as *invisible* or *that which is concealed.* He was usually depicted as a bearded man in the prime of life wearing a headdress with a double plume. Amun has been suggested as originally referring to the power of the wind.

Amun was a creator god, who gained solar qualities when fused with Re. He was also known as the Lord of Victory and Lover of Strength, showing martial aspects. In one form he was known as the Great Shrieker, as the primal goose who uttered the first sound and laid the world egg. As the ram-headed serpent Kematef (*"He who has completed his moment"*) he was also said to have created the world egg.

Amun also had an ithyphallic aspect as the bull, and can be seen as a fertility god. Amun was sometimes called the God who exists in all things, as the ba (soul) of all life, a view which leans towards monotheism. Lapis lazuli was sacred to Amun as the Lord of lapis lazuli due to its heavenly symbolism, and ammonite due to its shape.

Amulets	For eye ailments
Animals	Serpent, bull, ram (with curved horns), Nile goose, lion, bee
Colours	Blue, red
Concepts	Protector of the common man, protection from crocodiles, scorpions and other dangerous animals, fertility, invisibility, oracle, strength, wind
Symbols	Twin feather plumed crown, ammonite

Anubis

Anubis (or Anup or Anpu) means *Royal Child*, probably referring to the myths of his birth from the adultery of Nephthys and Osiris, the King. This was a later attribution however, as earlier texts have Anubis being the child of either Bastet or the cow goddess Hesat. Anubis was usually depicted as a jackal or wild dog-headed man, or a reclining black jackal. Anubis was the great protector god, guiding the soul through the underworld. He was also the Lord of embalming, and through this is connected with incense and perfumery.

In the New Kingdom Anubis was seen as being in charge of legions of thousands of daemons, and could be appealed to for protection against negative magic, especially curses. He also punished those who violated tombs or gave offence to the gods. In later depictions he was sometimes shown as a warrior with a serpent's tail instead of legs, and wearing armour. Along with Isis, Sirius was also sacred to Anubis as the Dog Star, though it has been suggested that Sirius B represented Anubis, and Sirius A was Isis.

Originally Anubis was the ruler of the underworld, a role which was taken over by Osiris. However his significance was never fully lost, hence he has titles such as Hery Seshta (Master of Secrets) and Wer-Hekau (Mighty One of Magic).

Amulets	Knotted threads called *Anubis threads* used to bind supernatural enemies
Animals	Jackal, Dog, Wolf, Cobra
Colours	Black, gold
Concepts	Protection from negativity and when travelling, finding lost items, guardian, incense & perfume, judgement, magical power, protection from curses, psychopomp
Symbols	Funerary knife, imiut, incense, leopard skin (to celebrate his victory over Set), Sekhem

Apophis

Apophis (or Apep) was the great chaos serpent who attacked the solar barque each night as it travelled through the underworld. His many epithets describe both his negative aspects, such as Evil lizard, Opponent and Enemy, as well as the necessity of his role, such as World encircler and Serpent of rebirth. The latter title refers to the myth versions where he swallows and disgorges Re each night and morning, renewed.

Apophis was also associated with natural events like earthquakes, storms and unexplained darkness (i.e. eclipses). One later version of the myths has Apophis created from the saliva of Neith, forming him as a serpent which is described as being 200 cubits long (about 111m).

Amulets	None, as he represented chaos.
Animals	Serpent
Colours	-
Concepts	Chaos, destruction, enemy, renewal
Symbols	-

Atum

Atum (or Atem or Temu) means *The Complete*. His name reflects the belief that Atum began the line of the gods and created the manifest universe. In different myths he did this by masturbating or using his saliva. Atum was called the Lord of Totality, and was said to have millions of ka's, which were every living thing, leaning (as with Amun) towards a monotheistic supreme deity.

Atum was usually depicted as a mature man in his prime, as it was believed to depict the gods as weak or old could influence them. Atum also represented the primeval mound that rose from the first waters of creation.

Atum was the progenitor of the Ennead line. He was often linked with Re, to form the supreme creator deity Atum-Re. The Eye of Atum was a term sometimes used to describe the more benevolent protective aspects of the Eye goddesses, commonly known as the Eye of Re. This term was also used to describe the Moon.

Amulets	-
Animals	Ram, serpent, eel, cat, mongoose, lion, bull, lizard, ape, scarab
Colours	Gold
Concepts	Creation, journey of life, protection from serpents and negative forces, setting Sun, totality
Plants	Ished tree
Symbols	The sacred stone (possibly meteorite)

Bastet

Bastet (or Bast or Pasht) has two possible meanings, Bas with a feminine ending, meaning *She who devours*, referring to the use of cats to protect the grain from rats. Alternatively Bastet means *She of the Bas-jar*. A bas-jar is a perfume jar, and Bastet was linked with hygiene.

Originally Bastet was a lioness-headed goddess, but with time she was depicted in the more familiar cat-headed form (from about 1000 BCE). Bastet was the protective mother but also the avenger, in one version of the myths she decapitated Apophis with a knife when he threatened the solar barque.

Bastet was one of the Eye goddesses credited with being the Eye of Re, and was sometimes considered to be the wife of Atum-Re, bearing him a child Mahes, a lion-headed god. Bastet was also often depicted as a cat, with kittens at her feet.

Amulets	Menat
Animals	Cat, lioness
Colours	Green
Concepts	Eye of the Sun, nursemaid, protection during pregnancy, avenging wrong, pleasure
Symbols	Sistrum, uat sceptre, utchat eye

Bes

Bes is probably derived from the word Besa meaning *to protect*. Bes was actually the most popular of a group of ten or so deities of ugly form (Aha, Amam, Bes, Hayet, Ihty, Mefdjet, Menew, Segeb, Sopdu and Tetetenu)) who were considered powerful protective gods. Bes was usually depicted as an ugly dwarf, often with leonine characteristics, a large erect penis and his tongue stuck out.

There was also a female form of Bes called Beset with similar qualities to him. Beset was shown as a dwarf with a more normal body, and also shown naked, demonstrating her sexual power and also to scare away hostile beings.

He was often shown strangling snakes, waving knives or playing musical instruments. Additionally he often displayed his large genitals to frighten other beings away. His hideous image could be considered the original prototype for medieval gargoyles.

Images of Bes were frequently carved on beds and their headrests to protect the sleeper, and also on mirrors, cosmetic and unguent jars, as all these items were frequently used in magic.

Along with Taweret, with whom he was sometimes partnered as husband, Bes was one of the major deities of protection for pregnant women. Bes was associated with love and marriage as well as childbirth, and was a deity of fun. Bes also became syncretized with other deities to create composite "super-deities" in the New Kingdom.

Amulets	Bes figurines for protection during pregnancy and childbirth. See also notes above.
Animals	Lion
Colours	-
Concepts	Protection during pregnancy and childbirth, protection when sleeping and from nightmares, exorcism, marriage, humour
Symbols	Knives, musical instruments, Sa symbol, wands

Geb

Geb means *Earth* or *Goose*. He was almost always shown as a man, reclining with a large phallus pointing straight up in the air. Geb's body was seen as being the physical earth, the planet beneath us, and the goose was one of his symbols. Unlike many later cultures the Egyptians depicted the earth as male.

Geb represented the power of the earth, both its fecundity and its wrath. His laughter was said to produce earthquakes, and he could withhold his blessings and make the land dry or barren. He was said to swallow up the dead and be responsible for the dangerous snakes that lived under the earth. Grain was said to sprout from Geb's ribs and vegetation from his back, making him the forerunner of other vegetation god figures right through to the Green Man.

Geb was also associated with kingship, which is not surprising as the king had to maintain a good relationship with the land he represented. Geb was also considered a powerful healing deity.

Amulets	-
Animals	Goose, hare
Colours	Green
Concepts	Fertile earth, earthquakes, vegetation, crops, healing, especially of scorpion stings, kingship
Plants	Pine
Symbols	Phallus, goose, vegetation

Hathor

Hathor's name means literally *The House of Horus*, indicating her role as alternatively mother or consort depending on which version of the myth you consider, and also linking her to the night sky as Lady of the Stars. She was usually shown as a beautiful woman wearing a red solar disk on her head between a pair of cow's horns.

Hathor was one of the goddesses referred to as the Eye of Re. She was called the Beautiful One, and was linked with female sexuality and motherhood. Hathor was also known as the Hand of Atum, Mistress of the Vagina and the Lady of the Vulva. The latter title refers to an incident where Atum was unhappy, so Hathor cheered him up by exposing herself so he laughed and rejoined the other gods. Music, song and dance, and drunkenness, were all associated with Hathor.

Hathor was also the patroness and protector of exploits in foreign lands, such as the mining of copper, malachite and turquoise in the Sinai. In this role she was also known as the Lady of Turquoise and this stone was considered sacred to her, as were all precious metals and gems. As mirrors were often made from polished copper, this may be where the association of the mirror with Hathor stemmed from, though its use to make oneself beautiful is also appropriate. Hathor was sometimes seen as being the personification of gold, and this is shown in her title The Golden One. Myrrh was also considered sacred to Hathor. Hathor was often depicted in a red dress, and was known as Mistress of the red cloth, which implies her power, due to the colour associations of red.

Hathor is referred to in multiple form as the Seven Hathors. In this form, they pronounced the fate of newborn children (ideal for name giving ceremonies!) as well as protecting them in the womb. The expectant mother would bind knotted red ribbons in her hair to protect her child until it was born. The Seven Hathors were also appealed to in love spells and their knotted red ribbons used to bind poisons and dangerous spirits.

Amulets	Menat
Animals	Cow, lioness, serpent, cat
Colours	Green, blue, red
Concepts	Beauty, binding poisons and dangerous negative influences, dance, female sexuality, love, motherhood, music, nurturing, pleasure, protection of influences abroad, song, trees
Plants	Sycamore, papyrus
Symbols	Horned solar disk, gold, mirror, myrrh, sistrum, turquoise, wine

Heka

Heka means *Lord of Ka's*, and he was the god of magic. He was depicted as a bearded man wearing a lion nemes headdress or as a young child with a solar disk on his head. One of his titles was The one who consecrates imagery, referring to the ability of the god to empower creative thoughts and actions and translate them into their physical equivalents in the physical world. He was frequently described as being the Ba of Re.

Amulets	-
Animals	Lion, serpent
Colours	-
Concepts	Magic, power, divinity
Symbols	

The God Heka is also explored in Chapter 1 of the current volume.

Heket

Heket (or Heqet) was a frog-headed goddess associated with childbirth, and later with assisting the Pharaoh to ascend when he had died. She was also depicted as a knife-wielding frog, usually on apotropaic wands. She was one of the deities popular with the people in folk magic, with amulets depicting her being frequently used to assist in pregnancy and childbirth.

Heket was also known as Mistress of Joy, and by the New Kingdom was being credited with giving birth to Re from the primeval slime, and being the divine midwife of the soul after death.

Amulets	Heket figurines for pregnancy and childbirth protection
Animals	Frog
Colours	-
Concepts	Childbirth, fertility, joy, primeval creation, resurrection
Symbols	Frog

Horus

Horus the Elder (or Harwer or Haroeris) was a protective god, whose name may mean *high* or *above*, or possibly *The Distant One*. He was usually depicted as a hawk-headed man or a hawk. Both the meanings of his name are very appropriate for the celestial falcon or hawk, soaring high above the earth, and clearly show the origin of his title Lord of the Sky.

Horus may originally have been a stellar god, with the speckles on his breast feathers representing the stars, his wings the sky and his eyes being the sun and moon. He is best known as a solar god, the Lord of the East. Emerald was sacred to Horus as the Prince of the Emerald Stone.

It may seem strange that there should be two separate gods called Horus, but how many friends do you know with the same name? So we have Horus the Elder, brother of Isis and father of the four Sons of Horus, and Horus as the son of Isis (Harpocrates) who grows up to avenge his father Osiris and defeat Set. This Horus, referred to as Horus the Younger, is also known as Hor or Heru. Harpocrates is referred to as Hoor-paar-Kraat in some modern texts, like Liber Al.

Horus was also associated with several of the planets. Venus, Mars, Jupiter and Saturn were all linked to different aspects of Horus.

Amulets	Cippi amulets for protection from snakes and scorpions
Animals	Falcon, falcon-headed crocodile, hawk
Colours	Gold, blue
Concepts	Sun, clear vision, kingship, planets (see above), protection, victory
Plants	Acacia, myrrh
Symbols	Winged sun disk, Eye of Horus

Hu

Hu means *creative utterance* or *annunciation*, and he was one of the deities responsible for the process of creation, embodying the great magical power of words, and the authority these give. He was said to have sprung from a drop of blood from the phallus of Re.

Hu was depicted as an anthropomorphic god in the solar barque. He is sometimes known as The One who speaks in the darkness, indicating his role in the process of creation.

Isis

The name Isis (or Aset or Isa) means *The Throne*. This goddess was depicted as a beautiful woman with a throne headdress, and was often depicted winged, though in later times she also assumed the horned sun disk of Hathor, whose role she largely took over. Isis was often shown kneeling on the hieroglyph for gold, which was linked to her through its funerary use.

In the Isis began to be associated with the Moon in the New Kingdom , but she has much earlier stellar associations, specifically with Sothis (Sirius). Apart from being the protective mother and loyal wife, Isis was also known as the Mistress of Magic, having gained Re's true name from him by trickery.

With her sister Nephthys, Isis was also involved in caring for the dead, and had a strong presence in the underworld with her husband and brother Osiris.

Pearls and carnelian were also sacred to Isis, the latter being called the blood of Isis.

Amulets	Tyet
Animals	Kite, cow, scorpion, serpent, sow
Colours	White
Concepts	Magic, cunning, determination, healing, loyalty, motherhood, protection especially of children
Plants	Sycamore
Symbols	Ankh, Sirius, Throne crown, uat sceptre

Khephri

Khephri (or Khepry or Khophri) means *He who came forth* or *He who came into being*, showing the spontaneous nature of Khephri's coming into being. He was often equated with Atum for this reason. Khephri was usually depicted as a beetle-headed man or as a scarab beetle.

The beetle's habit of pushing a ball of dung was equated on a cosmic scale with Khephri pushing the sun through the sky. He was equated with the dawn sun, with the title The Shining One, and this is also shown when Re tells Isis that he is *"Khephri in the morning, Re at noon, Atum in the evening"*.

Amulets	Scarab beetle
Animals	Scarab beetle, beetle-headed hawk
Colours	Black
Concepts	Regeneration, becoming, dawn Sun, overcoming corruption, transformation
Symbols	Scarab beetle

Khnum

Khnum (or Chnum) was often seen as the personification of the creative force of the Nile, as he was responsible for its inundation from its source. He was depicted as a man with the head of a long-horned ram. Khnum was frequently shown as a potter, who had shaped all life on his wheel, being the Maker of every body and Lord of the Wheel. He was also referred to as being the Ba (soul) of Re, and at times also of Geb and Osiris.

Khnum was sometimes paired with the frog goddess Heket. He was also paired with Neith, and called Lord of crocodiles, probably referring to the Nile and also Neith's son Sobek.

Amulets	Engraved for childbirth protection or Nile inundation
Animals	Ram, crocodile
Colours	Blue
Concepts	Creation, childbirth, creativity, inundation, pottery
Symbols	Atef crown, potter's wheel

Khonsu

Khonsu's name indicates his role as the moon god, coming from the verb khenes meaning *to traverse*, or *cross over*, i.e. *He who traverses the sky* or *The Traveller*. Although he was most often depicted in human form as a child wearing the sidelock of youth, Khonsu (or Khons or Chons) was also sometimes represented as being falcon-headed. His headdress was of a full moon above a crescent moon.

Khonsu was initially considered a ferocious figure, eating the hearts of the dead and keeping the *Books of the End of the Year*, which indicated who would die in the next year. Because of these qualities he was invoked for protection to deal with powerful demons.

Amulets	-
Animals	Falcon, baboon
Colours	
Concepts	Gestation, fate, mercy, Moon, time, protection from negative entities
Symbols	Full Moon disk, crescent shaped pectoral

Maat

Maat means *Truth*, and this goddess embodied the concepts of truth, justice and cosmic order. She is described in the Pyramid Texts as standing behind Re, implying that she is the source of his power. As time passed she became seen as the daughter of Re, and also as the wife of Thoth, God of Magic, who put the laws of Maat into writing.

Maat was usually depicted as a beautiful young woman with wings and her symbol of the white ostrich feather on her head. One of her symbols was the hieroglyph of the plinth on which statues stood, implying the supremacy of Maat, representing the order that even the gods strive to perceive. This may be seen through Maat shrines usually being present in the temples of other gods rather than being distinct, and also statements like "the gods live on Maat.

Amulets	-
Animals	-
Colours	White
Concepts	Truth, justice, cosmic balance, order, judgement
Symbols	White feather, heart

The Goddess Maat is also explored in detail in Chapter 2 of the current volume.

Min

The origin of Min's name is unknown, though Plutarch claimed it meant *that which is seen*. Min was the supreme god of male sexuality and procreativity. He was depicted as a cloaked figure with a large erect penis, with his right arm raised in a smiting gesture, sometimes wielding a flail or whip, and wearing a headdress with two large plumes.

The festival of Min, held at the beginning of harvest, was one of the major agricultural celebrations, and was known as the coming forth of Min, indicating a desire for the fertility in the crops that the god represented. Statues of Min were carried to the fields to bless and protect the crops, and the first fruits of the harvest would be offered to him.

There is much debate about the mysterious symbol of Min. It has been suggested that this is a lightning bolt, a belemnite, a barbed arrow or a door bolt.

Amulets	Figurines for male sexual potency
Animals	White bull, falcon, bee
Colours	Black
Concepts	Agricultural fecundity, fertility, male sexuality, protection when travelling
Plants	Lettuce
Symbols	Cos lettuce, Min emblem, phallus, flail

Mut

Mut (or Mout), whose name means *Mother*, became adopted as the wife of Amun, displacing his original consort. She was depicted as a mature woman wearing a vulture headdress. Egyptian queens associated with Mut, and her role was primarily in the realm of the living as a protective goddess. Interestingly she is the only goddess shown wearing the combined double crown of Upper and Lower Egypt.

Mut was seen as a southern counterpart of Sekhmet, being another of the goddesses regarded as an Eye of Re. Her flames were greatly feared, and rebels and traitors were burned alive in the brazier of Mut. Mut was well known for her temple oracle, and was highly venerated by many Egyptians.

Amulets	Depict Mut as protective mother
Animals	Vulture, lioness, cat
Colours	Blue, red
Concepts	Motherhood, oracle, protection, punishment of traitors, sovereignty
Symbols	Twin crown of the Two Lands, twin sceptres, vulture

Nefertem

Nefertem (or Nefertum) means *The Beauty of Tem*, indicating the fact that he was also sometimes seen as a younger aspect of Atum (Atem). He was depicted as a young boy sitting on a lotus. He was also shown as a mature male with a lotus blossom on his head, or a headdress with two upright plumes around a lotus, and two necklaces hanging down. A few images show him as a lion-headed god, reminding us of his mother Sekhmet.

Like Bastet he was linked with perfumes. Nefertem was the lotus that helped the sun (Re) rise in the mornings, and he is also called The lotus blossom which is before the nose of Re. The metal silver was associated with Nefertem.

Amulets	Protective amulets for child at birth
Animals	Lion
Colours	White
Concepts	Male beauty, perfumery, rising Sun
Symbols	Blue lotus, Khepesh sickle-sword, lotus headdress, perfume, silver

Neith

Neith (or Neit) was one of the earliest of the Egyptian gods, identified with the primal waters of Nun, and was seen as a Creatrix. Her name may mean *The terrifying one.* She was usually depicted as a beautiful woman wearing the red crown of the north. According to one text Neith created both Re and Apophis, as well as mankind.

Neith was a war goddess, with titles like Mistress of the Bow and Ruler of Arrows. Neith was another of the ferocious goddesses who could be a manifestation of the Eye of Re, and would strike down his enemies. The red crown of Lower Egypt was also known as the Net (Neith) crown, showing her importance.

Amulets	Child protection, shown nursing crocodiles at her breast or as a crocodile-headed woman.
Animals	Cow, crocodile, serpent, bee, beetle
Colours	-
Concepts	Creation, mother, power, victory, war
Symbols	Bow, crossed arrows, harpoon, was sceptre

Nephthys

Nephthys (or Nebt-het) means *Lady of the House*, referring to the portion of the sky that was considered the abode of Horus. Nephthys was the dark twin of Isis, sharing the role of protecting Horus with her. She is depicted as a beautiful woman, with the symbols of her name making her headdress.

She is mainly known as a funerary goddess in the underworld, being one of the main protectors of the dead. Nephthys has come to be associated with being unseen (invisible).

Amulets	-
Animals	Kite
Colours	Black
Concepts	Invisibility, motherhood, protection
Symbols	Linen bandages

Nuit

Nuit (or Nut) means *Sky*. Nuit was the personification of the heavens, and was usually shown as a woman arched over the heavens, her body deep blue with golden stars in it, or as a giant cow with stars in the body. Her laughter was the thunder and her tears the rain. Evidence suggests that Nuit may originally have represented the Milky Way, for in pre-dynastic Egypt the Milky Way would have appeared like an arched figure. Lapis lazuli as symbolically representing the night sky was sacred to Nuit.

Amulets	Represented as a sow, as a fertility and rebirth figure
Animals	Cow, sow
Colours	Blue and gold
Concepts	Nourishment, regeneration, the universe
Plants	Sycamore, fig
Symbols	The 5-lined Star

Nun

Nun means *Primeval waters*, and Nun represented the primordial chaos from which Atum was formed. To the Egyptians this was an infinite expanse of water from which creation sprang, and this is later adopted into Judaism and Christianity (Genesis I.2 – *"And the Spirit of God moved upon the face of the waters"*). In some respects Nun was more of a place than a God, which continued to exist outside of creation.

Amulets	-
Animals	-
Colours	Blue
Concepts	Primal waters
Symbols	Mud brick wall enclosures around temples

Osiris

The original meaning of Osiris (or Asar) has been lost, though it may be derived from Useru meaning *Mighty One*. He was usually depicted mummified, carrying a crook and flail, and with black or green skin. Osiris wears a very distinctive crown, known as the Atef crown, which is the conical white crown of Upper Egypt, framed with tall red plumes (representing Busiris, the centre of his worship) and ram's horns, showing his virility.

The star Orion was sacred to Osiris, and the pyramids were aligned with it. The number seven was also sacred to Osiris, as the number of days he spent in the womb of his mother Nuit. Multiples of seven occur around Osiris, e.g. his body being cut into fourteen parts (2x7), and the forty-two gates in the Underworld (6x7).

Osiris was originally a vegetation god, who gave man corn and the ability to cultivate it, and also wine. He also taught man animal husbandry, and was well-loved. The black Nile mud, vital for the fertility of the land, symbolised Osiris as the fertile god, in his union with Isis as the flowing waters of the Nile. After his death, with the loss of his penis he becomes Lord of the Underworld, no longer fertile, but in a more significant role.

Osiris is shown carrying the crook in his left hand as a symbol of divine authority and government, and also showing his link to humanity as their shepherd, receiving them into his kingdom after death. In his right hand he carries the flail as a symbol of his divine authority. The flail was a symbol of kingship, carried by the pharaohs to identify them with Osiris. A variant of this position of the arms (though crossed) has survived through the ages and is called the Osiris position in modern magic.

Amulets	Djed
Animals	Bull, wolf
Colours	Black, green, blue
Concepts	Lord of the Underworld, divine judge, kingship
Plants	Willow
Symbols	Atef crown, corn, crook and flail, djed pillar, false beard of kingship, Sekhem

Ptah

The meaning of Ptah is uncertain, though it is possible it means *Sculptor*. This would fit with his role as God of craftsman and divine architect. Ptah was depicted as a bearded man wearing an artisan's skull-cap and a cloak, with blue skin, being known as He who is beautiful of face. Ptah was also the patron of arts and smithing. In some of the myths Ptah was seen as the creator of the universe.

Ptah was said to have created the opening of the mouth ritual used to make statues fit vessels for deities to manifest in, and for mummification. Ptah as He of the hearing ear held an interesting role as *hearer of prayers* for the ordinary people as well as nobility. Ptah's sceptre was a combination of the ankh, the djed pillar and the was sceptre.

Amulets	As a dwarf on Cippi for healing, as a Djed pillar in the Old Kingdom.
Animals	Bull (the Apis bull was said to be the ba of Ptah)
Colours	Blue
Concepts	Arts, crafts, hearing, metalwork, pottery, prayer, sculpting
Plant	Moringa tree
Symbols	Ptah sceptre, skull cap, straight beard

Re

The meaning of Re (or Ra) is uncertain, but it has been suggested as *Sun* and *Creator*. The journey of Re (the sun) through the sky was one of the foundations of Egyptian daily life, making Re arguably the most important god. Atum and Ra were often linked as they were both creator gods. Re's form changed – in the morning he was depicted with the head of a scarab beetle, through the day he was falcon-headed or the solar disk, but during the night he was often shown as ram-headed.

Re acted within five roles – as a deity of heaven, earth and underworld, as a creator and as protector of the Pharaoh. The Eye of Re was an epithet given to various goddesses in the role of destructive avenger of slights to Re. Gold as the solar metal (reflecting the brilliance of the sun) was sacred to Re, who was sometimes called The mountain of gold. Both tiger's eye and topaz were sacred to Re, probably due to their solar colouring.

Amulets	For veneration, and to right wrongs
Animals	Bull, cat, child, falcon, hawk, heron, lion, phoenix, ram, scarab, serpent, vulture
Colours	Gold, red
Concepts	Sun, creation, order, protection, regular travel, Regulus (the star)
Symbols	The Sun, Eye of Re, flying vultures, mound, obelisk, protective cobra, pyramid, solar barque, Sun disk, yellow bands

Sekhmet

Sekhmet (or Sakhmet) means *powerful female*. This is entirely in keeping with Sekhmet as the personification of the heat of the midday sun (Re, her father), and destroyer of demons and pestilence. She was depicted as a lioness-headed woman, wearing a wig and solar disk, with a uraeus serpent at her brow.

Sekhmet was believed to ride in her chariot to war with the Pharaoh, ensuring victory for Egypt in battle. Sekhmet was usually depicted wearing the Uraeus crown, showing her power. She was thought to breathe fire to burn the enemies of Sekhmet, and if a person somehow got burned, they would make offerings to Sekhmet to appease her for whatever they had done to upset her. The hot desert winds were sometimes called the "breath of Sekhmet".

Sekhmet was also known as the Lady of the Red Linen, a very similar title to Hathor, with whom she was strongly linked, often being seen as two parts of the same goddess. Ruby was the sacred stone of Sekhmet, its hardness and red colouring being indicative of her nature.

The Seven Arrows of Sekhmet were hurled at people by her to bring them misfortune (often as infectious diseases) if they had angered her by disrespecting her father Re. They had a positive use as well in warding off the evil eye. Sekhmet was also known as the Mistress of Life, and her priests were noted healers.

Amulets	Figures of Sekhmet
Animals	Lioness, cobra
Colours	Red
Concepts	Strength of the midday Sun, divine retribution, fighting the Evil Eye, fire, healing, misfortune, especially infectious diseases, setting bones, victory in battle
Symbols	Chariot, Leo (constellation and sign), rosettes, Sekhem, seven arrows, sistrum, uat sceptre, Uraeus crown

Serket

Serket (or Serqet or Selket) was a very early deity, associated with protection, and often paired with Neith. Her name in full was Serket Hetyt, meaning *She who causes the throat to breathe*. She was also seen as a mother goddess, as the scorpion was associated with motherhood. Although she was usually depicted with a scorpion on her head with raised tail, the scorpion was never drawn complete or sculpted complete, for magical reasons, to ensure the benevolent healing aspect of the goddess rather than the destructive one.

Amulets	Scorpion amulets to protect from poisonous bites and stings
Animals	Scorpion, crocodile, lioness, serpent
Colours	-
Concepts	Childbirth, motherhood, protection, rebirth
Symbols	Scorpion

Seshat

Seshat means *female scribe*, and this describes her role as goddess of writing. One of her titles was She who is foremost in the house of books. Seshat was often depicted wearing a leopard skin, and with a headband surmounted by a seven-pointed star or rosette that was unique to her.

Her role encompassed accounting, census taking, libraries, and all forms of notation, and she was the patroness of architecture, astronomy and mathematics. Seshat recorded the deeds of men and gods on the Tree of life.

Amulets	-
Animals	Leopard
Colours	-
Concepts	Writing, astronomy, building, knowledge, mathematics, record-keeping
Plants	Persea tree
Symbols	Seven pointed star/rosette headdress, leopard skin, stake and mallet (for measuring), stylus

Set

The origin of Set's (or Seth's) name is uncertain. It may come from the word setken meaning *to dazzle*, or setes meaning *stabilising pillar*. The latter name would fit with Set's role as holder of the ladder for Horus to ascend to heaven. Set is a very misrepresented god. Set represented the destructive forces of nature, like the fierce desert wind, flash floods, sandstorms and earthquakes.

He was also a deity of chaos. The Egyptians feared chaos, so to combat the forces of chaos, as represented by entities like the chaos serpent Apophis, they needed a god who also partook of the nature of chaos. Thus it was Set who killed Apophis and saved the gods on the solar barque when they were hypnotised by Apophis. Although Set was feared, he was also respected, and every Pharaoh had a name associated with Set.

Set was known as great of strength and Lord of metals. Iron was known as the bones of Set due to its use in making weapons.

Amulets	Gems engraved with Set were used to prevent miscarriage and heavy bleeding
Animals	Set beast, fenekh fox, antelope, ass, bull, crocodile, hippopotamus, leopard, oryx, panther, pig
Colours	Red
Concepts	Non-conceptual sex, including homosexual sex, dealing with negativity, desert, fighting demons and chaos, iron-working, sea, strength, untamed force of nature, violence
Symbols	Ursa Major, giant mace, iron, Set beast

Shu

Shu (or Schu) probably comes from the root word shu meaning *dry* or *He who rises up*.   Shu represented the air, and he was positioned between Nuit (heaven) and Geb (earth) to separate them by a jealous Re, as the winds and the air.   Shu was also associated as light, which may have been seen as a function of air.   In the early texts Shu was sometimes equated with Maat.

Amulets	Shown supporting the sun disk, for protection from poison
Animals	Lion
Colours	-0
Concepts	Air, light, renewal, wind
Symbols	Feather

Sia

Sia means *perception*, and with Hu and Heka, he forms the triad of magical deities whose energies are central to practising magic. Sia was sometimes said to be in the eye of Re, enabling him to understand all that goes on in the world, and was also known as the one who speaks in darkness, showing his role in the primaeval creation.

Like Hu he was said to have come from blood from the phallus of Re. Sia is described as being at the right hand of Re, and carrying his book. He was also linked with Ptah as being his ba. Like Hu he was also depicted as an anthropomorphic figure in the solar barque, and he gives the orders to open each of the twelve gates of the underworld on the nightly journey of the solar barque.

Sobek

The name Sobek (or Sebek) simply means *crocodile*. He was a powerful deity of fertility, both procreative and vegetative. He was also seen as deity of might, and as the son of Neith this is understandable. Sobek was said to have a temple of carnelian, so this stone can be seen as sacred to him. Sobek is shown as a crocodile or a crocodile-headed man wearing the Sun Disk with horns and plumes, and was called green of plume indicating his fertile nature.

Sobek was honoured as a god of water, and became the patron of fishermen. In some accounts the Nile is said to come from his sweat. In later times Sobek was sometimes associated with Set as being a form of the latter god.

Amulets	Depicting Sobek for fertility and protection
Animals	Crocodile
Colours	Green
Concepts	Fertility, might, vegetation, water
Symbols	Sun disk with horns and plumes, water

Sothis

Sothis (or Sopdet) was the personification of the star Sirius, which heralded the vital inundation of the Nile. As a result of this she was known as the Bringer of the New Year. Sothis was portrayed as a woman with a tall crown with tall upswept horns at the side, with a five-pointed star on top. These significant attributions of the pentagram and the star Sirius have become major themes of modern magic.

Her husband was Sah, who personified Orion. This couple were later largely absorbed into Isis and Osiris, who subsequently had the attributions of these stars to them. One story has Sothis uniting with Osiris to subsequently give birth to the planet Venus.

Amulets	-
Animals	Cow, dog
Colours	Blue
Concepts	Inundation, guide, mother, nurse, Sirius
Symbols	Five-pointed star, Sirius

Taweret

Taweret (or Tauret) means *The great female one*, and she was particularly associated with protection of pregnant women and childbirth. She was usually depicted as a hippopotamus with pendulous breasts, lion's paws and a crocodile tail, wearing a female wig. She sometimes had a feathered headdress or solar disk and horns surmounting the wig.

Amulets	Protective depictions for safe childbirth
Animals	Hippopotamus, cat
Colours	-
Concepts	Childbirth protection, protection, water
Symbols	Ankh, Sa symbol, flaming torch

Tefnut

Tefnut probably comes from the words teftef and nu meaning to *moisten* and *waters*. As the goddess of moisture and the morning dew her name is very descriptive, and in later texts was represented by a pair of lips spitting. Tefnut was another of the goddesses who could be the Eye of Re.

Tefnut was usually shown as a lioness-headed woman, with a female wig and a solar disk and uraeus serpent on her head. She was also sometimes depicted as a rearing serpent on a sceptre, or a lion-headed serpent (an interesting image for anyone interested in Thelema).

Amulets	-
Animals	Lioness, serpent
Colours	-
Concepts	Dew, moisture, saliva, water
Symbols	Lion-headed serpent, Uraeus

Thoth

Djehuty (Thoth) means *Leader*. Thoth was the God of magic and writing and gave many gifts to mankind like beer, bread and writing. Thoth was most often depicted as an ibis-headed man, or sometimes as an ibis or a baboon (the Ape of Thoth). In some of the myths Thoth created the universe through speaking. Thoth was originally a moon god. He was noted for truth and integrity, giving rise to the phrase that a person had lived his life straight and true like Thoth.

Thoth was patron of scribes, who made a libation from the water pot they dipped their pens in at the beginning of each day. The lunar metal silver was particularly associated with Thoth, as was emerald, which he was said to have given to mankind. Thoth was said to have been born from the lips of Re, or from the forehead of Set after he had swallowed some of Horus' semen.

Amulets	As Ibis or Baboon to aid in writing or magic
Animals	Ibis, baboon
Colours	Green
Concepts	Magic, fate, messenger, writing, precognition, incorruptibility, truth
Symbols	Moon, ibis, silver, stylus

Wepwawet

Wepwawet (or Upwaut) translates as *Opener of the Ways*, a phrase that has a number of connotations. It could refer to the opening of the mouth ritual performed on the deceased, leading the deceased through the underworld, leading the Pharaoh to conquest, or opening the sky for the sun to rise.

Wepwawet had a martial aspect, as a warrior he aided the Egyptian army in battle. He is often confused with Anubis, but is usually portrayed grey rather than black, and always in jackal form, usually standing on a standard rather than reclining. The two gods correspond to the north (Anubis) and south (Wepwawet) of Egypt.

Amulets	-
Animals	Jackal
Colours	Grey
Concepts	Beginnings, psychopomp, punishment, strength, war
Plants	Tamarisk
Symbols	Bow, mace, shedshed (royal placenta)

Composite Deities

Syncretism was a common practice in ancient Egypt. Different gods were often combined into a single form, in recognition of the interconnection of different divine forces, or indeed manifestations of a single divine force.

Ammut

Ammut means female devourer of the dead, and she is best known as the devourer of souls, of those whose heart did not balance the feather of Maat on the Scales of Judgement. Ammut was a composite mythical creature, essentially an underworld goddess. She had the head of a crocodile, the neck, mane and forelegs of a lion (or sometimes a leopard) and the rear legs of a hippopotamus.

Horakhty

This falcon-headed crocodile was the fusion of Horus with another god, possible Sobek.

Horbes

This complex deity was a combination of Horus, Hathor, Re and Bes.

Hormakhu

This deity was a composite of Horus and Thoth, depicted as Horus. He combines the solar-martial qualities of Horus with the magical qualities of Thoth. He is also referred to as Hrumachis (in Liber Al).

Mut-Sekhmet-Bast

A terrifying composite triple-headed winged goddess. She was depicted with the heads of a woman, a lioness and a vulture, and also had a penis. She was invoked for protection from a horrible death.

Ptah-Sokar-Osiris

This composite deity symbolised the cycle of regeneration. Ptah was the creator, Sokar the metamorphosis of death and Osiris the rebirth. He was sometimes shown presiding over the judgement of the dead in the Hall of Two Truths.

Re-Harakhte

This hawk-headed god combines the qualities of Re and Horus of the Akhet, making a sort of super-solar deity. He is also referred to in more modern times as Ra-Hoor-Khuit (in Liber Al). Re-Harakhte was usually depicted with blue skin, his associated colour.

Sut-Hor

This deity was depicted as Horus, with Set's head coming out of his neck in the opposite direction. Sut-Hor combined the qualities of these two opposing deities, dark and light in balance.

The Bes "Super-God"

The role of Bes as a protective deity comes to its climax in the composite Super-God. This seven-headed Bes is a god who the magician specifically identifies with to draw on the ba's, the spiritual essences of different gods contained within this composite deity (including Amun, Min and Horus), and he does not hold a place within the pantheons as such. He also has four pairs of wings. It is described in a magical papyrus:

> "The Bes with seven heads ... It embodies the ba's of Amun-Re, ... lord of the sky, the earth, the netherworld, the water and the mountains, who keeps his name mysterious before the gods, the giant of a million cubits, the mighty one who fastens the sky on his head, [...] from whose nose the air emerges to give life to all noses, who rises as the sun to brighten the earth, from the effluxes of whose body the inundation flows to give life to every mouth." [10]

Another version of the figure has nine heads and two pairs of wings. Amongst the heads are those of 'evil' creatures, showing this magical figure represents all the different energies. It stands upon an oval with a serpent ouroboros. The accompanying text describes the figure:

> "With nine faces on a single neck, a face of Bes, a face of a ram, a face of a hawk, a face of a crocodile, a face of a hippopotamus, a face of a lion, a face of a bull, a face of a monkey, and a face of a cat." [11]

---

[10] *The Origin of the Bes Image*, J.F. Romano, 1980.
[11] *The Origin of the Bes Image*, J.F. Romano, 1980.

4. Other Spirits

Bau

Bau were manifestations sent by a deity if someone had offended them. A Bau would cause misfortune to occur in someone's life, and they would have to find out who they had offended and make reparations to bring life back to normal. In the Late Kingdom Anubis is referred to as the Lord of the Bau, and was often appealed to in such circumstances to help sort the problem out.

Demons

The denizens of the underworld were often fearsome, with animal heads and ferocious weapons, but they were not seen as evil. Such beings could be appealed to for help, or might be directed by a deity to exercise their divine displeasure. It is important to realise they were seen more as spirits than negative beings.

Mut

Not all the spirits of the dead made it to the Fields of Reeds. Some types of spirit were denied entry, and might then return to the land of the living as the mut, the dangerous dead (no connection to the goddess Mut). The mut included the spirits of those who had been denied proper funerary rites, traitors, prisoners of war, people who had died violent deaths or very young, those whose heart failed at the balance, and those who had failed to achieve their aims whilst on earth. There were many spells and charms available to protect the living from the wrath of the dead, who were believed to be very magically powerful.

PART II
SYMBOLISM

5. The Symbolism of Colours

The use of colour in Egyptian magic is of primary importance. To the Egyptians, living in a largely bleak, desert landscape, bright and vibrant colours were a way of enriching their lives. The Egyptian hieroglyph for colour can also be translated as being, character, disposition, nature or external appearance. This clearly illustrates the significance of colour as being an essential and integral part of the Egyptian worldview.

When depicting groups of people or animals, the Egyptians usually alternated the colour on them, to give a sense of perspective. Hence the colour will often alternate between two shades, light then dark, in pictures of groupings.

The main colours used by the Egyptians were:

Black

Black (*kem*) was the colour of night, and of death. Black symbolised the underworld, but could also symbolise resurrection, life and fertility. In this respect black was interchangeable symbolically with green. This association probably comes from the fertile black silt of the Nile, deposited in its annual flooding and ensuring the fertility of the land. Egypt itself was known as the black land (*kemet*). Black was also interchanged with blue for representing the night sky.

Black was associated with funerary deities such as Anubis and Osiris, interchangeably with green in the latter case. In the later Macedonian and Ptolemaic periods black stones were used almost exclusively for magical healing statues. Carbon from soot, charcoal or burnt animal bones was used to produce black.

Blue

Blue (*irtiu* or *khesbedj*) was used to represent both the heavens and the waters. Both these symbolisms are those of life and rebirth, the eternal sky and the annual flooding of the Nile, which recalled the primal flood of myths. Blue was also associated with fertility, as the power of the fecundating Nile river, so vital for the crops the ancient Egyptians depended on. As well as being interchangeable with black for the heavens, blue was also interchanged with black as an underworld colour.

Blue was associated with Amun-Ra, and sometimes with Osiris. Ptah, Horus, Khnum, Re-Horakhty and Nuit were all often depicted with blue bodies. The Eye of Horus amulets were most often blue, symbolising their heavenly power. The blue pigment was formed by combining iron and copper oxides with silica and calcium.

Green

Green (*wadj*) was the colour of growth and of life itself, a life-positive colour seen in the plants that sustained the culture through food, medicine and writing (the papyrus). To do green things was a term used to describe good deeds.

In some early texts the afterlife is referred to as the Field of malachite, and green came to be associated with resurrection through the annual return of the green plants. Osiris as Lord of the Underworld was usually depicted with green skin, and Hathor was also associated with this colour. Copper oxide or malachite was used to make the colour green for artwork.

Red

Red (*desher*) was seen as the colour of blood and fire, and could symbolise life and regeneration. Red also represented the forces of chaos, and dangerous powers outside of man's control. Red was specifically associated with Set, as was red hair. Red also represented the untamed vastness of the desert, and sometimes foreign lands as dangerous places.

Red ink was used to write the hieroglyph for evil, and for the demon or unlucky days. To do red things was to perform evil acts. However, red was also used to depict Re, and the fierce radiance of the sun. Red was used to colour the Eye of Re serpent amulet. The red colour was created by using oxidized iron and red ochre.

White

White (*hedj* or *shesep*) was the colour of cleanliness, associated with sacredness and ritual purity. Clothing, especially that of the priesthood, was usually shown as white. This is well illustrated by the *Instructions of Merikare*, where the term wearing white sandals is used to describe being a priest. Many of the sacred objects were made from white alabaster, and many of the sacred animals were also white, such as oxen, cows and hippopotami.

White was also used interchangeably to describe silver, which was sacred to the Moon. The crown of Upper Egypt was known as the White crown, and white was the heraldic colour of southern Egypt. The god Nefertem, whose symbol was the white lotus flower, often had his statues made of silver, to illustrate his link with the colour white. Chalk and gypsum were both used to give a strong white colour.

Yellow

Yellow (*khenet* or *kenit*) and gold were the colours of the sun, and symbolised eternity and constancy. The ancient Egyptians believed the flesh and bones of the gods were made of gold, and so it was a natural progression to see yellow and gold as sacred colours, and to use gold in the construction of statues of the deities. The Egyptians had several sources of yellow, ochre and imported orpiment (arsenic trisulphide) being the most commonly used.

Other Colours

Brown, grey, orange and pink were also sometimes used, but as only secondary colours. Such colours were formed by adding white or black to the primary colours, or mixing them accordingly.

6. Sacred Numbers

Although we shall consider all the main numbers that occur and their relevance to practitioners of Heka, it should be noted that certain numbers occur repeatedly in Egyptian magic, and are used frequently in the repetition of spells and invocations. These numbers are two, three, four and seven, which can be seen as the major numbers. It is interesting to note the absence of five and six as major numbers to the ancient Egyptians.

One - Creation

One is the number of creation, the original monad that divides into plurality. Understanding this perception is vital to practising Egyptian magic. This is why different deities can be seen as the creator in different myths and different times and not be seen as clashing. It is also why many of the deities could be seen as androgynous, with greater emphasis subsequently given to the masculine or feminine side, such as Atum and Neith. Likewise it also illustrates how a composite deity can be seen as being one containing the energy of several.

Two – Duality as Manifested Unity

Although two represents duality, the Egyptian worldview held duality as the complementary aspects of unity. Hence two also implied one as the greater whole. Heaven and earth, day and night, the Sun and Moon, all are seen as parts of the essential unity of all things. It is essential to see the division as being part of a greater whole and not as polar opposites.

Nowhere is this better illustrated than in the crowns of Upper and Lower Egypt, where the red crown of Lower Egypt fitted inside the White crown of Upper Egypt to give one symbol of rulership and divinity. The sexual symbolism of the crowns is also quite apparent, and emphasises why Egypt is known as the home of alchemy.

The unity of all was expressed through the two forms of eternal sameness (*djet*) and eternal recurrence (*neheh*). This sharing of opposites to create a unity is also seen through the pairs of deities throughout the Egyptian cosmology. So from the four pairs of primal male-female deities in the Ogdoad, through to the classical Ennead pairs, such as Shu-Tefnut, Nuit-Geb, Isis-Osiris and Nephthys-Set, the greater whole is expressed through duality.

The same dual expression of the greater whole is seen in heaven-earth, light-dark, sun-moon (the two eyes of heaven), and through perceptions of humanity, e.g. man-woman, young-old, small-tall, etc.

It would perhaps be an easier representation in modern perceptions to think of the duality in ancient Egyptian thought as that of binary (base 2), 0 and 1, rather than duality, 1 and 2. For the whole binary system hints at hidden concepts and mysteries, best illustrated through that most important of stars to the ancient Egyptians, Sothis (Sirius).

The Egyptians knew that Sirius B, although hidden, orbited Sirius A as part of a binary system, and that the rising of this star system on the horizon would herald the Nile flood. Though one star was hidden, the 0 as it were, both were known to influence the most essential occurrence of the Egyptian calendar.

Three - Plurality

Three was the number of plurality for the ancient Egyptians. This is clearly shown in the hieroglyphs, where groups of three images are used to represent plurality, which in later times became simplified to three vertical lines (| | |). Three is also a crucial religious number, as the deities were repeatedly grouped into triads of father, mother and child, e.g. Osiris/Isis/ Horus, Ptah/Sekhmet/Nefertem or Amun/Mut/Khonsu.

The other key religious use of three is in the fusing of gods to make a trinity of triune combination. The best example of this is the three creator gods Amun, Re and Ptah being seen as part of the great whole. A 19th Dynasty document says *"All gods are three ... Amun, Re and Ptah."* Re represented the face, Ptah the body, and Amun the ba, or hidden soul. The other classic example is the fusing of Khephri, Re and Atum to represent the sun as the morning, noon and evening.

Three also represents cycles, as the three seasons of the year (akhet, peret and shemu – the time of inundation, the time of emergence, and harvest), and the three ten day periods that each of the twelve months was divided into. Prayers and sacrifices were usually offered three times.

Four - Completion

Four occurs incredibly often in both art and ritual. Groups of four are very common, such as the four sons of Horus, the four funerary Goddesses, four animals, etc. Four is tied into the cardinal points, and this is a natural development in a country with the north-south axis of the Nile and the east-west axis of the sun's journey. The four quarters of heaven are frequently referred to, through such visual images as the four legs of the cosmic cow.

Four is used frequently in ritual, especially for censing and purification. Words would be spoken at each of the cardinal points for completion and strength.

Protection rituals also often involved protective items being put at each of the four quarters, and four protective deities being stationed at the quarters. Priests were expected to bathe four times a day – twice in the day and twice in the evening. The universe itself was also divided into four areas – earth, sky, heavens and underworld. Four represented the totality of all, as the complete union of all forces.

Seven - Perfection

Seven was often associated with perfection. This may be because it was the union of the two great numbers three and four. Many deities had sevenfold aspects or manifestations, such as the seven Ba's of Re, the Seven Hathors, the seven Arrows of Sekhmet. Seven scorpions accompanied Isis on her journey to find the dismembered parts of Osiris.

Seven was frequently used in healing spells. Seven knots are often tied in cords for dealing with health problems, and seven sacred oils were also used in embalming. Multiples of seven occur frequently in Egyptian myth and magic as well. Hence Osiris was cut into fourteen parts (2x7), there are forty-two gates and forty-two judges (6x7) in the underworld, where the forty-two Negative Confessions are spoken, the moon waxes and wanes through twenty-eight days (4x7).

Eight

Eight does not occur with the same frequency as the major numbers, yet it still has symbolic relevance. Eight represents an intensification of the totality of four, by doubling it. Hence we see the Ogdoad of eight primeval deities (four gods and four goddesses) who precede creation.

Nine

In the same way as eight, nine represents the plurality of three intensified, by multiplying it by itself. Nine also referred to deities, with the Ennead of Heliopolis being the nine deities of the line of Atum (Atum, Shu and Tefnut, Geb and Nuit, Osiris and Isis, Set and Nephthys). Nine is used to represent an all-encompassing group.

Ten

Ten was connected with time and space, and their measurement. Groups of ten occur in the months (three ten day periods), and a generation was held to be thirty years (3x10). If a Pharaoh ruled for thirty years he had to undergo purification rituals to ensure he was fit to reign for the next generation. The ideal length of life was said to be 110 years, or 10x10+10. Spaces were often measured out in multiples of ten units (e.g. cubits).

Twelve

As with ten, twelve ties in mainly with time. Hence the twelve hours each of night and day, and the twelve months of the year.

7. Symbols (common)

A number of symbols were widely used by the ancient Egyptians. Many of these are covered in the chapter on tools and the appendix on amulets and talismans, but a few of the most important symbols are covered below.

Ankh

No-one knows exactly where the ankh came from, but we do know that the concept of life associated with the ankh encompassed life-sustaining waters, air, food, life-force and sexual fecundity. Many libation jars and vessels were made in the shape of the ankh, as it was thought the power of the ankh would bless the water within and make it more powerful. You can pour water or wine through the loop of an ankh as a form of blessing.

Sexual fertility was also linked to the ankh, which represented sexual union as the combination of the pubic triangle (as the loop), and the penis as the line below uniting with it. The ankh is also known as the key of life. The word for mirror was the same as that for ankh, suggesting the need to look truly at oneself and not fall prey to delusion.

Figure 5 : The Ankh

Ben-ben

The ben-ben was a cone-shaped rock, possibly originally meteoric in origin, which represented the manifestation of the primeval god from the waters. The ben-ben was a primitive obelisk, said to be the prototype of the pyramids.

Benu Bird

The Benu bird was said to be the oldest living creature, and was closely associated with Re. The cry of the benu bird was said to be the point at which time began. The phoenix was derived from the benu. Initially described as being like a yellow wagtail, it was subsequently depicted as looking like a heron. The Benu was very fond of perching on the ben-ben stone.

Djed Pillar

The hieroglyph for the Djed pillar meant stability. Originally the Djed may have been a pillar of corn sheaves or reeds, but it came to represent the spine of Osiris. The Djed may also have been seen as an axis mundi, uniting the earth with the sky.

Lotus

The blue lotus was associated with creation, coming into being at the time of creation from the primeval waters. It was associated with the sun, and also used widely for decoration. Additionally it had narcotic qualities that may have been used for ritual purposes.

Sphinx

The sphinx was a mythical creature, with the body of a lion and the head of a man or woman (usually the reigning king or queen). Female sphinxes were often depicted with wings. These sphinxes embodied the power of the ruler and their duty to defend Egypt and uphold Maat. Other sphinxes were shown with the heads of hawks, rams or the Set beast, and guarded temples and tombs.

A double sphinx called the Aker guarded the entrance and exit to the Underworld. Another sphinx with wings and a snake tail was called Tutu, and was considered to be one of the goddess Neith's offspring. Tutu was invoked to keep enemies at bay.

Uraeus

The Uraeus was a spitting cobra, worn by royalty as a crown at the brow to denote their rank and protection from enemies. It symbolised the power of the Eye goddesses who embodied the Eye of Re.

Utchat Eye

The Eye of Horus is one of the best known Egyptian symbols. It is also known as the udjat or wedjat eye, and it was formed when Set and Horus were fighting over the kingship. Set pulled out Horus' left eye and threw it away. The Eye landed on Thoth's wing, who spat on it and restored it to Horus. Horus then offered the Eye to his father Osiris in an act of filial devotion, helping restore him to life.

There were actually two Eyes, which symbolise the sun and the moon, depending on whether they face right or left. When it faces right as the sun it was also known as the Eye of Re.

PART III
PREPARATION

8. Tools Used

Apotropaic Wand

These wands were used to control or banish spiritual beings, especially negative entities. They were made of tusk ivory, and generally shaped like a boomerang. Apotropaic wands were carved with animals. Apotropaic wands were sometimes used to mark out a sacred circle on the floor for working magic within. They were also placed on or near the bed at night to protect the sleeper whilst they slept.

Figure 6 : Apotopraic Wand

Bow

The bow was a symbol of power, especially sacred to Neith. It also represented the enemies of Egypt, who were referred to and depicted as the "Nine Bows". As it is not easily used as a ritual item it is included here for informational purposes.

Clappers

Pairs of carved ivory clappers, similar in appearance to apotropaic wands were used to make noises to drive away evil spirits. By carving different animals onto the clappers the power of the animals would thus be translated into the clappers.

Cosmetic Spoon

Often decorated with similar symbols to those found on mirrors, these spoons were used in a ritual context. This may have been for offering things (incense, food, drink).

Drum

Drums were used to frighten away demons, often in conjunction with masks such as those of Bes or Hathor.

Fan

Fans symbolised the breath of life, and are often seen depicted in conjunction with the ankh. The fan also represented the shadow, as it cast shadow itself. The fan moved air, and so could be used in conjunction with incense for censing.

Knife

The word for knife is the same as that for flint, *des*, showing the link between the stone and the weapon. Knives were a symbol of protection and retribution. Malevolent creatures were often shown in images being cut with knives to render them powerless, giving a good example of the use of the knife.

Mirror

Mirrors were generally made of polished bronze, and usually in the shape of the solar disk with a handle. Mirrors were particularly associated with Hathor and often decorated with her face. They were also decorated with images of Bes, falcons, lotuses and lilies.

Rod

Cylindrical or rectangular rods of ebony or glazed soapstone were used as a symbol of authority and power. These would be used more for summoning entities. These also often had animals carved onto them, and sometimes figures of magical animals set on top, like lions or crocodiles.

Sekhem Sceptre

As with other wands and sceptres, the Sekhem represents power and authority. It carries with it the connotations of command, and hence might be used to command ethereal beings. The Sekhem was associated with Sekhmet, Osiris (as Great Sekhem) and especially with Anubis. The Sekhem was held in the right hand and the staff or incense burner in the left when officiating at rituals, and would be waved over the offering items four or five times as the recitations were made.

Figure 7 : Sekhem Sceptre

Serpent Wand

Serpent wands, with a cobra on the end were used as a symbol of authority and kingship. They imposed order onto chaos, and commanded supernatural creatures.

Sistrum

The sistrum is uniquely Egyptian. The Egyptian name for the sistrum is *sesheshet*, derived from the name for papyrus, as the sistrum is thought to have originated from the practice of shaking bundles of papyrus flowers (seshen) in honour of Hathor. There were two types of sistrum, the hooped sistrum and the naos sistrum. The hooped sistrum has a hoop on the handle with small metal disks or squares set on rods in the hoop. The naos sistrum differs from this in the setting of twin Hathor heads in a small shrine (naos) between the handle and the hoop. The naos sistrum was often decorated with uraeus serpents and connected to the symbolism of the snake. The sistrum was associated with protection, divine blessing, and rebirth.

Figure 8 : Hooped Sistrum   Figure 9 : Naos Sistrum

Was Sceptre

The Was sceptre was a straight shaft with a forked bottom, with a transverse diagonal top, shaped as the head of a fantastic beast, most often the Set beast. The Was represented power and dominion, and was most often shown with the ankh and the djed. The Was sceptre was often carried by deities, and might be used for priestly work manifesting the energy of a deity the magician is linked to.

Figure 10 : Was Sceptre

Robes

The robes worn by the Egyptians are well depicted in the inscriptions and papyri we have been left. Men usually wore a simple wrap-around kilt on white cotton.

Sandals

Sandals made of reeds were usually worn. Leather was not worn due to the taboos regarding animal items.

Myrrh Ink

A recipe for myrrh ink is given in the Greek magical papyri, many of which were derived from Egyptian sources. That this one is can be seen by the inclusion of the ibis. Mix the following ingredients:

> 4 drams (14g) Myrrh resin
> 3 figs
> 7 date stones
> 7 dried pinecones
> 7 piths of wormwood
> (7 wings of the ibis)
> Spring water

A simple recipe can be made using modern ingredients. This is made from acacia (gum Arabic), myrrh oil, soot, distilled water and burned peach kernels.

9. Sacred Words

The magic of words is central to heka, and to Egyptian civilization as a whole. Words were considered inherently magical, and this is why saliva, which came into contact with the spoken words, was considered magically powerful. The Egyptian name for their system of writing was *medu netcher* meaning *the words of the gods*, or *divine words*. The Greek word hieroglyph (*sacred writing*) preserves something of this intense importance attached to both the written and spoken word.

The Egyptians made a clear distinction between ordinary speech and writing, and crafted literature, which they called beautiful speech. Certain features stand out which can be used as guidelines for constructing invocations in the ancient Egyptian style.

One common technique is the use of thought couplets (technically known as distichs), where the second sentence expands or rephrases the theme of the previous sentence. This also occurs with tristichs, on a three line theme. Of all Egyptian literature hymns of praise or worship stand out as the most carefully composed and descriptive.

A good example of this is the *Hymn to the Inundation* written by Khety during the Middle Kingdom period.

> *"Worshipping the Inundation.*
> *Hail to you, Inundation,*
> *Who emerges from the ground and comes to make the Black land live;*
> *Hidden of conduct, dark in the daytime,*
> *To whom his followers sing;*
> *Who waters the fields that Re creates,*
> *In order to make all the flocks live;*
> *Who states the hills that are far from water,*
> *Whose dew is what comes from the sky;*
> *Whom Geb desires, who manages Nephri,* [12]
> *Who makes green the craft of Ptah."* [13]

---

[12] Nephri was a grain god.
[13] Reproduced in *Middle Egyptian* by James P. Allen, p341.

Letters to the Dead

Another means of written communication was to write letters to the dead. If a person felt they had been wronged, they could write a letter to the dead, asking them (with their strong heka) to intercede on their behalf. The letter, usually written on a bowl, would be placed next the food offerings so the spirit would find them when it came to partake of the essence of the food. It is possible this practice may have also been performed orally, making spoken requests when presenting food to the ancestors.

The letters usually consisted of five parts. These were the address, greeting, praise of the deceased to encourage assistance, statement of the wrongdoing, and appeal for help. If you wish to use this technique to ask an ancestor or dead relative for help, this is the template you should use.

The following is a classic example of a letter to the dead, on a bowl in the Louvre, from a woman called Merti to her deceased son Mereri. It is interesting to note that the dead are expected to already know details of the wrongdoing, as these are usually only briefly described.

(Address)
"O Mereri, born of Merti."

(Greeting)
"The god Osiris-Khentamenti assures that you shall live for millions of years, by providing the breath in your nose and by placing bread and beer by the side of Hathor, lady of the horizon. Your condition is like [one who] lives millions of times by order of the gods who are in the sky and on earth."

(Praise)
"You make obstacles to enemies who have evil characters [and who are] against your house, against your brother, and against your mother [who loves] her excellent son Mereri. You were excellent on earth and thou art beneficent in the land of the dead. Invocations and offerings are made for you. Bread and beer are placed upon the altar of the god Khentamenti.[14] *You sailed downstream in the night-barque [of the Sun God]; you sailed upstream in the day-barque [of the Sun God]. You are justified in front of every god. Make yourself my favourite dead person!"*

---

[14] Although originally a god in his own right, Khentamenti (foremost of the westerners) became absorbed into Osiris, who is clearly referred to here in this context.

(Wrong)

> *"You know that he said to me, "I shall report against you and your children."*

(Appeal)

> *"You report against it; you are in the place of justification!"* [15]

An example of the appeal from the Old Kingdom describes how the spirit might work in the Appeal section of the letter:

> *"Please become a spirit for me before my eyes that I may see you fighting on my behalf in a dream."* [16]

Body Art

Body art occurs in ancient Egypt in more than one form. Hieroglyphic images of divine beings and protective signs were sometimes drawn onto the skin in ink. These might then be licked off, transferring the heka of the spell into the body and further empowering it with saliva.

Magicians sometimes painted the feather of Maat onto their tongues, so that they would only speak words of truth and uphold Maat with their actions. It has been suggested that illustrations showing figures with designs painted on their bodies represent tattoos, and certainly it is known that women sometimes had tattoos of the dwarf god Bes to increase their fertility or improve their sex life.

---

[15] *Ancient Egyptian Magic* by Bob Brier.
[16] *Offerings: An Overview*, by G. Englund.

10. Sacred Gesture

As the images we have show people frozen in postures, much of the information about sequences of gestures is speculative. What we do have is images of certain types of posture, which may be incorporated into personal practice. As you will see, kneeling was considered a sign of respect, and thought to intensify the feeling conveyed in some of the gestures. The postures fall into eight categories – dominance, invocation, mourning, offering, praise, protection, rejoicing and submission

Dominance

This includes positions such as with a raised weapon, signifying the destruction of foes. Standing with feet on the necks or backs of enemies can be seen as another version of this, as could trampling one's enemies.

Invocation

This is the gesture of summoning. This is made with an arm outstretched, bending it in slightly with the hand held palm upwards to the vertical. The other arm is held vertically next to the body. This gesture is shown in the hieroglyph *nis* meaning to summon.

Figure 11 : Nis Posture

Mourning

This is relevant only for funerary depictions but included here for completion. The mourning gesture has one or both arms raised before the head as if to cover the face, or actually placed on the top of the head. If only one arm is raised the other is held next to the body, as shown in the hieroglyph *iakbyt*, meaning mourning woman. Again the gesture is intensified by kneeling.

Figure 12 : Iakbyt Posture

Offering

Being the position used for the presentation of objects. This is done with the object being held in an outstretched and cupped hand. This is shown in the hieroglyph *derepi* meaning *to offer*.

Figure 13 : Derep Hieroglypic

Praise

This is usually made towards the gods. The sequence known as the *Recitation of the Glorifications* is depicted by the hieroglyph showing the final gesture (*henu*).

Figure 14 : Henu Posture

You kneel on one knee, with knee and toes touching the ground, and the other foot touching the ground. The arm on the same side of the body as the kneeling knee is extended at a horizontal or slightly upward level, with the elbow bent at a right angle and hand open. The other arm is held back with closed fist towards the body.

As the recitation continues the raised arm is drawn back to the horizontal and the hand closed into a fist. You then touch or strike the chest with alternate fists. At the end of the recitation you should return to the original posture. The beginning and end posture is demonstrated in the hieroglyph *henu*, meaning praise.

Adoration is also expressed through the posture depicted by the hieroglyph *dua*, meaning adore. The arms are held next to the body with the elbows bent at an angle of about 60°-70° to the vertical, and palms open facing downwards. Although the hieroglyph shows one arm in front of the other, this can be seen as an artistic technique to display perspective, as all the statues in this posture have the arms in exactly the same position. This posture could be made standing or kneeling.

Figure 15 : Dua Posture

Another gesture can be made by raising one or both arms up horizontally to shoulder level, with palms facing outwards towards the object of praise (seen in the hieroglyph *dua*). When this gesture is made kneeling rather than standing it shows greater intensity and means greater praise is being given.

Protection

This is depicted by stretching out one or two fingers (the index, or index and large fingers) towards the source of danger. Shown in pictures being made towards dangerous animals like crocodiles.

Rejoicing

This is used when celebrating victories or receiving rewards. One or both hands are held palm outward above shoulder level. This is shown in the hieroglyph *hai* meaning rejoice.

Figure 16 : Hai Posture

Submission

This is a gesture of respect. Submission gestures include movements such as bowing whilst touching one or both hands to the knees, and/or grasping one or both arms or shoulders with the opposite hands.

Other Gestures

Anointing

This was usually performed with the little finger outstretched and the rest of the fingers curled into the palm, the little finger having been dipped in oil, milk or other liquid.

Clenching the hand

This gesture was seen as a symbol of action – taking and holding, and hence represents creativity and power. This is shown in the hieroglyph for clenched hand – *khefa*.

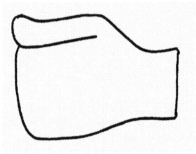

Figure 17 : Khefa (Clenched Hand)

Dominance

This was the classic pose of Osiris with the flail and crook is taken to be one of authority and dominance, and may be used accordingly.

Removing the foot

At the end of rituals the magician would practice removing the foot. This was the action of stepping backwards, sweeping away all footsteps. By this he leaves the shrine in its original state, symbolically returning it to the time of creation.

Supporting

This was when clear support for a person or object is given. This is done with arms outstretched touching the person or object.

11. Sacred Movement

As well as gesture, we also need to consider the practice of circumambulation, or walking around the boundaries. This practice was used in funerary rites from the early Kingdom, and subsequently in the Middle Kingdom in spells to protect the house, which would be walked around, and in the New Kingdom in similar rituals to protect the bedroom.

This action may also give us the root of the serpent ouroboros, which stems from ancient Egypt. A Middle Kingdom text says:

> *"It is the protection of Him who bends the knee in the Great Mansion who goes about surrounded in his protective serpent."* [17]

Giving a clear image of a protective serpent encircling a space. This is clearly illustrated by an image in the funerary papyrus of Herweben.

Indeed a temple dedication ritual at Edfu has the priests circumambulating the temple to purify it, protect it from external forces and delimit its sacred space and cosmic geometry. Ultimately this circumambulation is expressed of course by the journey of Re in his solar barque each day.

The act of encircling could also contain negative forces within. When Set defeats the chaos serpent Apophis he declares:

> *"I am the Great One of Magic, the son of Nuit. My magic (heka) has been given to me against you …. I have encircled the sky, while you are in bonds."* [18]

---

[17] *Egyptian Mythology*, Geraldine Pinch, 2002.
[18] *Seth, God of Confusion*, H. Te Velde, 1967.

Figure 18 : Ouroboros

12. Statues & Masks

The ancient Egyptians loved their statues! By carving an image in stone, it would ensure it would last for eternity. As the gods themselves were vulnerable to death, their depictions needed to be enduring. This is why carvings always show the gods as being larger, to indicate their divinity, and also enemies and creatures of chaos as being smaller. Beings such as Apophis were literally belittled in their images, to reduce their power. This magical technique is one that pervades ancient Egypt. Likewise scenes depicting chaos triumphant were never shown, which is why there are no carvings showing the death of Osiris.

The Egyptians practised a form of fetishism, believing that deities could inhabit their statues. As a result of this, great care would be taken to dress the statues each day and say prayers to the statues. By doing this the statues was made a fitting vessel for the god to reside and bring their energy into their temple.

Prayers would be said to statues, and they would be washed with clean water. Often they would be anointed, and dressed with jewellery and even clothes. Food and drink would also be offered to statues, as it was believed the deities could partake of the essence of them. These practices were also believed to help encourage the deity to manifest within the statues.

The number of texts referring to the deities entering their statues leave no doubt that this was part of the perception of how the universe worked. And it was not just the statues, but their representations that could be divinely inhabited as well. An example regarding Hathor from Dendara illustrates this beautifully:

> "She flies down from the sky to enter the akhet of her ka on earth,
> She flies down onto her body, she joins with her form.
> She unites with her forms that are carved in her sanctuary.
> She alights on her forms that are carved on the wall." [19]

When a statue was dressed, the first thing done was the removal of the cloth it had been left in from the previous day for purification. The purifications with water and incense would then take place. The statue would then be dressed in four different types of cloth in turn. First white to safeguard it from its enemies, then blue to hid the face, then green for bodily health, then red for protection. The little finger would then be dabbed in ointment and lightly touched to the statue's forehead. The priest would then retreat erasing his footsteps.

---

[19] *The Mechanics of Ancient Egyptian Magical Practice*, R.K. Ritner, 1993.

From around 2000 BCE statues of the Pharaohs were also used in magic. Petitions were made to these statues to act as intermediaries with the major deities, in a similar way to the Catholic technique of praying to Saints to intercede for the individual.

An important consideration with Egyptian statues is the perception of temples to the ancient Egyptians. Temples were complex symbolic models of the cosmos. They acted as an interface between the human and divine worlds, providing houses for the gods to dwell within. The care of the statues can thus be seen as of paramount importance. At times the statues would be moved outside, e.g. statues of Re would be brought out to greet the dawn, so the metaphysical manifestation (the sun) could be joined with the statue as a spirit home for Re.

Opening of the Mouth

The Opening of the Mouth ceremony was performed on new statues of the gods from the very early periods onwards. Later it was adapted and used for mummies as well. The basic principle behind the ritual is to animate the statue, and allow it to function as a vessel for the deity. Though it would only be performed on a statue once, it was critically important. As animal sacrifice was part of this process, I have bracketed the actions that are not appropriate for modern times.

The ritual is recorded in the *Pyramid Texts*, spell 199:

- The statue is placed, facing south, on a mound or bed of clean sand.

- The statue is given a preliminary censing. The statue is sprinkled with water from two sets of four containers, representing the gods and goddesses of the cardinal directions. (East: Serket; South: Isis; West: Neith; North: Nephthys)

- The statue is presented with 10 pellets of natron and 5 pellets of incense.

- (2 oxen, 2 gazelles, and a duck or goose are sacrificed, and the heart and foreleg of one of the oxen presented to the statue.)

- The magical tools are touched in turn to the mouth of the statue, ears and eyes. This included a chisel and the ceremonial knife. These would be made of flint or meteoric iron.

- The mouth of the statue would then be anointed with fresh milk.

- The statue would then be clothed with appropriate garb.

- Anointing with precious oils would then take place.

- Jewellery would be placed on the statue.

- A meal would then be offered to the statue.

Masks

Apart from their use in funerary rites, masks were also used in magic to embody the power of deities, usually for protective rituals to scare off demons or restless ghosts.

Lion masks of the god Bes were sometimes worn by magicians for protection spells, possibly during protection rituals for people or places from malefic influences. They seem to have been worn for use with musical instruments for driving away evil spirits.

Hathor masks were usually two-dimensional, i.e. flat, with cow ears on the cow face. Some were bi-frontal, with the same face on the back as well as the front. Wigs were usually worn with Hathor masks. Masks were made of cloth, of wood, and of stone (steatite). Some were glazed with faience. It seems likely that these masks were worn to symbolise rebirth and the sexual nature of Hathor.

13. Sacred Materials

Crystals & Minerals

The Egyptians used a wide range of crystals and stones for building, and for tools, vessels and amulets.

Agate
Agate was used for jewellery and for amulets.

Alabaster
Alabaster was used mainly for producing bowls, lamps and vases, and considered particularly good for religious items due to its delicate coloration. Mainly quarried in Middle Egypt and the Sinai.

Amazonite
Amazonote was used for amulets and talismans. Some of the chapters of the Book of the Dead were carved specifically on amazonite.

Amber
Amber was used for jewellery.

Amethyst
The Ab amulet was often made of amethyst. Egyptian ambassadors carried a piece of amethyst when travelling abroad for protection.

Ammonite
This was used in the worship of Amun-Re (where their name comes from) due to the way they are shaped ie. like a ram horn.

Aquamarine
This was used in amulets and jewellery.

Azurite
Azurite was used for amulets to provide insight and visionary powers.

Basalt
Black basalt was widely used for making statues, sarcophagi and pavements. In the later periods healing statues were sometimes made of basalt.

Beryl
Beryl was used for jewellery.

Breccia
Both green and the red and white varieties of breccia were used occasionally for making vases and other stone objects.

Calcite (Iceland Spar)
Calcite was used for jewellery.

Carnelian
This stone is widely known as the Blood of Isis, and was used for jewellery and amulets. The Tyet was often made of carnelian, as were the Tet and the Ab, and chapters of the Book of the Dead. Master architects wore carnelian as a badge of rank, and soldiers for courage and to overcome their enemies.

Chalcedony
Chalcedony was used for jewellery.

Diorite
This green stone with white or black coloration and speckles or banding was quarried in Nubia and used to make bowls and other fine quality objects, including occasional beads for necklaces.

Emerald
Emeralds were used mainly for amulets, including the Uat. Emerald was sacred to Thoth as representing spring was said to have been given to man by him. It was also sacred to Horus.

Faience
This is a gritty material made from powdered quartz fused together with an alkali and glazed, usually in blue or green. It was cheap and widely used for jewellery.

Flint
This was used especially for ceremonial knives and blades.

Garnet
Garnet was used for jewellery and amulets.

Granite
The black, grey and pink varieties of Granite were all available to the Egyptians, who used it for buildings, sarcophagi and statues.

Haematite
Haematite was used in amulets and medicinally to treat inflammation and hysteria. The Neha and Urs amulets were usually made of haematite.

Heliotrope
This was used ground up with honey in medicine to stop bleeding. Amulets made of heliotrope were thought to make the bearer renowned and famous, and protect him from deception.

Ivory
Hippopotamus ivory was used in apotropaic wands due to the great strength and magical associations of the hippopotamus. It was also widely used in jewellery and sometimes for votive statues.

Jasper
Both red and green jasper were used. The Tyet amulet was often made of red jasper, as were serpents-head amulets for protection from snake bite in the underworld. The Ab was sometimes made from green jasper. Green jasper was considered exceptionally powerful as an amuletic stone.

Lapis Lazuli
This beautiful stone was highly prized by the Egyptians who considred it to be the stone of heaven. The hair and beards of the gods were said to be made of lapis lazuli. Lapis lazuli was used mainly for jewellery and amulets, especially scarabs, Utchat eyes and the Ab. Lapis lazuli was crushed to make ultramarine pigment for use in eyeshadow.

Malachite
Malachite was used in jewellery and also crushed for use in eyeshadow.

Marble
This was widely used for building and statues.

Obsidian
Obsidian, a volcanic glass, was used for tools that needed to be sharp like knives, due to its hardness.

Onyx
This was used in jewellery and amulets for cooling the ardours of love.

Pearl
Pearls were sacred to Isis and used in jewellery.

Peridot
This stone was worn by some priests to keep their minds clear of envy or jealousy.

Quartz
Quartz was used for amulets, jewellery and votive statues.

Quartzite
This hard form of sandstone was used for buildings and sarcophagi, and could be white, yellow or red, giving it solar connotations.

Rose Quartz
This stone has been found in funerary masks. Powdered it was thought to be good in cosmetics used to treat and prevent wrinkles.

Sand
Mention should also be made of the most common material of all in ancient Egypt – sand. Sand itself was used in a wide range of ways. It was ritually strewn during processions, offered to deities, used to clean a space, added to statues and used as a base for images, bowls and lamps. It was also used in spells for blinding enemies and repelling demons.

Selenite
This stone was cut into egg shapes known as Pharaoh's Eggs which were thought to bring protection.

Serpentine
Serpentine was widely used for small objects. Because of its patterning, it was frequently used for amulets to ward off snake and scorpion attacks.

Shell
Cowri shells were widely used in jewellery, especially in girdles and collars for women.

Sodalite
This was used in amulets for strengthening the mind and dispelling fear.

Steatite
Steatite (also known as soapstone) was widely used for amulets and making vessels as it is easy to shape and carve.

Tiger's Eye
This was used on statues to decorate and represent the eyes. Tiger's Eye was believed to enable the bearer to see everything, even through walls. It was sacred to Re.

Topaz
This stone was used in jewellery and sacred to Re.

Turquoise
Turqoise was highly prized for jewellery and amulets. Green turquoise symbolised fertility and resurrection.

Metals

The ancient Egyptians had already discovered metal-working in the pre-Dynastic period, c. 5000 BCE, and at that time were working copper, gold, lead and silver. The planetary attributions of copper, gold and silver to Venus, the Sun and Moon probably originated in Egypt, as these associations are already demonstrated by the linking of the metals to particular deities.

Antimony
Beads dating to 800 BCE have been found, made from antimony, which were probably traded from the Assyrians.

Bronze
From the 3rd Dynasty bronze is first used, though it was not common until the Middle Kingdom, allowing for the making of much harder and more durable tools.

Copper
From pre-Dynastic times copper was used to make tools. In 1st Dynasty tools a small amount (about 1%) of bismuth has been found, which would make the copper harder.

Electrum
This amalgam of silver and gold was used for jewellery.

Meteoric Iron
Used for ritual items due to its scarcity and origin as coming from the sky. It was known as *bia-en-pet* or metal of heaven, and seen as having great magical potency.

Lead
Also used from pre-Dynastic times for small statuettes, plaques and love charms, and in the New Kingdom for curse tablets (via Graeco-Roman influence).

Pot Metal
An alloy of copper and lead used in the New Kingdom for making statuettes.

Silver
The Egyptians called silver white gold, and it was much rarer than gold. Silver was linked with the moon, and sacred to Thoth. It was also associated with Nefertem.

Gold

The bones of the gods were said to be made from gold, and it was widely used in jewellery throughout Egyptian history. As the divine and imperishable substance, gold reflected the brilliance of the sun. Gold was particularly linked with Re, Hathor and Isis.

Woods

The Egyptians imported much of the wood they used for doors, furniture and temple pylons. They were very fond of fine cedar from Lebanon, but used a number of other woods as well. These include:

Acacia, cedar, cypress, date palm, ebony, elm, fir, oak, persea, pine, sycamore, thorn, willow, yew.

Acacia was a favourite; the seeds were hollowed out and used for jewellery, especially girdles.

14. Incense and Perfumes

Incense

Incense played a major role in ancient Egypt. From pre-Dynastic times fragrant resins were placed in burial sites. Incense was seen as pleasing to the gods, and a way to connect the people to the gods, offering their prayers on the fragrant smoke that literally fed the deities.

Papyrus Salt 825 describes how incense came into being, from the gods:
> *"Horus cried. The water fell from his eye to the earth and it grew. That is how dry myrrh came to be. Geb was sad on account of it. Blood fell from his nose to the ground and it grew. That is how pines came to be and resins came to be from their fluid. Then Shu and Tefnut cried exceedingly. The water from their eyes fell to the ground and it grew. That is how incense came to be."* [20]

So passionate were the Egyptians about their fragrances that they went on the first recorded botanical expeditions in history to gather balsam, frankincense and myrrh trees to plant in their own lands so they would not have to rely purely on imports for their precious fragrances.

These expeditions were organised to Punt at the southern end of the Red Sea, starting with King Assa in the 11th Dynasty (circa 2000 BCE). When the Pharaoh Empress Hatshepsut led an expedition in the 18th Dynasty (circa 1500 BCE) it was recorded that she was personally involved, *"Her Majesty herself is working with her hands. The most precious myrrh is all over her body."* [21]

The trees were carried with words like the following to encourage them to prosper in Egypt:

> *"Myrrh tree come with us,*
> *Come to the land of the gods, to the kingdom of Amun.*
> *This is where you belong.*
> *You will thrive like Maat in the temple of Amun."* [22]

By burning incense it was believed to bring the gods close, hence the daily burning of incense in the temples and in homes. And of course incense had the added bonus of keeping insects away! As the ancient Egyptians said, *"A day without fragrance is a day lost"*.

---

[20] *Le Papyrus Salt 825*, P Derchain.
[21] *The Complete Incense Book*, S Fischer-Rizzi, 1988.
[22] *The Complete Incense Book*, S Fischer-Rizzi, 1988.

The Journey of Re

Different fragrances were burned during the day to indicate the journey of Re through the heavens. At dawn when the sun rose frankincense was burned. At midday when the sun was at its peak they burned myrrh. At sunset when Re descended into the underworld they burned Kyphi.

In Medicine

The use of incense is well documented in the medical papyri as well as the magical ones. Injured parts of the body were exposed to incense smoke, and it was also used to drive away the demons believed to cause some of the illnesses.

Visionary Incenses

Some of the recipes recorded used psychoactive plants, for inducing visions in the priests, or for temple sleep for people being healed or dream visions. The ingredients included blue lotus, datura and poppy in a frankincense base.

Common Incense Ingredients

The ancient Egyptians used the following substances for their fragrances. If you are practising Heka, these are the scents you have to work with if you wish to strive for accuracy.

Aquillaria Wood (Aquillaria agallocha Roxb.)
Imported from Northern India, this fragrant wood was a popular ingredient in recipes like Kyphi.

Avar Tree (Tetraclinis articulata)
The resin of the Avar, known as sandarac was used both as an incense ingredient, and for its medicinal qualities.

Balsam (Balsamodendron gileadensis Knth)
Balsam is also called Mecca Balsam or Balsam of Gilead. It was imported from Judea and used for perfumery and embalming, and was imported at huge cost, around twice the weight of the resin in silver.

Benzoin (Benzoin Sumatra-Styrax Benzoin Dryand.)
Imported from India, Benzoin was used for incenses, representing joy with its sweet scent. Benzoin was usually mixed with other ingredients, probably due to its sharpness when burned alone.

Calamus (Acorus calamus L.)

Calamus root was used as an ingredient in Kyphi, and also for keeping the home clean. The fragrance of calamus was also considered a symbol of male potency, so it may be used for rituals emphasising the masculine.

Cedar (Cedrus libani, A. Rich.)
Cedar was very popular in ancient Egypt, especially the cedars of Lebanon. Cedar was used in mummification, and in incense for its associated quality of permanence.

Cinnamon (Cinnamonum zeylanicum Breyn.)
Cinnamon bark and dried blossoms were imported from Arabia. The antiseptic and antibacterial properties of cinnamon were well known to the Egyptians, who used it frequently for medicinal purposes as well as in incense recipes.

Cocoa Grass (Cyperus rotundus L.)
The roots of this grass were dried and added to incense recipes to give it a long-burning fragrance, as it burns very slowly – a very useful quality for incense!

Coriander (Coriandrum sativum L.)
The warm spicy fragrance of coriander was popular in Egypt, and the seeds were one of the ingredients of Kyphi.

Frankincense (Boswellia carterii Birdw)
The Egyptians believed that the phoenix took frankincense to the land of Punt in its claws. The hieroglyph for frankincense translates as becoming godly, indicating its pre-eminence of all Egyptian scents. Frankincense may be used for any rituals.

Galbanum (Ferula galbaniflua Boiss)
The Egyptians imported galbanum from Aisa Minor, and called it Mother resin, as it was usually used as a base for incenses mixtures.

Henna (Lawsonia inermis L.)
Imported from Cyprus and Sidon for use in Kyphi and other recipes. Although we may initially think of henna for its red dye, the flowers are very fragrant and were widely used in incense.

Juniper (Juniperus phoenicea L.)
The Egyptians used all parts of the juniper in their incenses – berries, twigs and wood. It was a symbol of longevity due to the age the trees grow to, and was widely used in incenses, including Kyphi.

Labdanum (Cistus creticus L.)
Labdanum resin was imported from Crete for its use in Kyphi and other incense blends, for its complex and sweet fragrance.

Mastic (Pistacia lentiscus L.)
Mastic was imported from the Greek island of Chios. As well as being an ingredient in Kyphi it was burned individually for its cleansing properties, being called the fragrance that pleases the gods.

Myrrh (Commiphora myrrha Nees)
Myrrh was said to have been created by the tears of Horus. The hieroglyph for myrrh (bal) translates as driving out insanity. Myrrh was considered to be very sensually stimulating, and associated with eroticism and love. It was also used for getting a good night's sleep. Physicians used myrrh for wounds and internal treatments.

Oponax (Commiphora Erythraea v. glabrescens)
Opoponax is also known as Sweet or Bisabol Myrrh. Opoponax was thought to shield against disasters. It was also though to help increase intuition.

Pine Resin (Albies alba Mill.)
Pine resin was usually collected during the Dog Days, when the weather was hottest and the water content correspondingly lowest.

Sandalwood (Santalum album L.)
Imported from India, the fragrant sandalwood was an important ingredient in Kyphi, and used for other incenses as well.

Spikenard (Nardostachys Jatamansi)
Imported from the Himalayas via India, the roots of spikenard were used in some incense mixes, including some versions of Kyphi.

Storax (Liquidambar orientalis Mill.)
Storax was imported from Asia Minor via the Phoenicians. It was called miniaki, meaning festive fragrance. Storax was burned to help people sleep well.

White Cedar (Thuja occidentalis L.)
White cedar was found in the tomb of Tutankhamen, and it is thought it was burned before the tomb was closed, possibly to help on the underworld journey.

The Use of Natron

Natron is a mineral salt used for purification and in embalming. It is worth trying to get hold of some if you are planning on seriously practising heka as it was very widely used.

15. Incense Recipes

You may wish to make your own incenses based on the Egyptian recipes for use in your practices, so here are some common recipes.

Cleansing Blend

Add equal parts of ground cinnamon bark to ground calamus root for an incense for cleansing a space before ritual, or for getting rid of negative influences.

Creativity Blend

If you are in need of creative inspiration, add 3 parts frankincense to 1 part each of myrrh and Benzoin for an inspiring blend.

Dreaming Blend

This blend was used as a perfume and also for inspiring dreams. Add 1 part each of calamus, myrrh, opoponax and storax (see note below on storax), and 2 parts each of cinnamon bark, frankincense and mastic. When making this blend, please ensure that the woody ingredients are well ground.

Mental Strength Blend

A mixture for mental strength and self-realisation is equal parts of calamus and storax. Storax can be tricky to use, so heat the sticky liquid storax over a candle flame until it is runny and then add the ground calamus to it before it sets.

Temple Blend

A common temple mixture for general ritual is Benzoin, cinnamon, frankincense and myrrh. These may be mixed in equal parts for a general-purpose incense for ritual use.

Kyphi

Kyphi was the favoured incense of the Egyptians. It took months to make Kyphi, with prayers and rituals accompanying its creation. Different sources give different versions of the recipe, with between 10-16 ingredients. The word Kyphi is a Greek transliteration of kapet, meaning incense.

Although Kyphi is mentioned in the *Pyramid Texts*, the first recipe for its preparation is in the *Ebers Papyrus* (c. 1500 BCE), where nine ingredients (mostly unidentifiable) are boiled in honey.

Carvings on the temple walls at Edfu give two recipes for Kyphi, and there are also carvings at Philai with a recipe. All give the same ingredients, but with different proportions, calling it the twice-good perfume.

The instructions, giving metric weights and added instructions for convenience, run as follows:

> *"Take 273 g each of mastic, pine resin, sweet flag, aspalathos, camel grass, mint and cinnamon. Place the items in a mortar and grind them. Two-fifths of this will be in the form of liquid to be discarded. There remain three-fifths in the form of ground powder. Take 681g each of cyprus, juniper berries, pine kernels and peker (unidentified). Reduce the ingredients to powder. Moisten all these dry ingredients with 935g (red) wine in a copper vessel. Half of this wine will be absorbed by the powder, the rest is to be discarded. Leave overnight. Moisten the 1498g raisins with 935g oasis (red) wine. Mix everything in a vessel and leave for five days. Boil to reduce by one-fifth. Place 1498g honey and 1213 g frankincense in a cauldron and reduce volume by one-fifth. Add to the honey and frankincense the kyphi macerated in wine. Leave overnight. Grind the 1155 g myrrh and add to the kyphi."* [23]

The Greek physician Dioscorides gives the following variation in 1st century CE:

> *"Kyphi is a mixture of incenses dedicated to the Gods. Egyptian priests use it very often. It is also mixed with antidotes and is given in beverages to the asthmatic. There are many methods of preparation, one of which is the following: half a xestes (0.137l) of galingale; the same quantity of the major juniper berries; twelve mnai (5239.2g) of big stoned raisins; five mnai (2183g) of cleansed resin; one mna (436.6g) each of sweet flag, aspalathos and lemon grass; twelve drachmai (48g) of myrrh; nine xestes (2.466l) of old wine; two mnai (873.2g) of honey."*

> *"Stone the raisins and chop them, and grind with wine and myrrh. Then grind and sieve the other ingredients and mix them with the aforementioned mixture. Let steep for one day. Then boil the honey until it thickens and mix thoroughly with the melted resin. Mix*

---

[23] *The Complete Incense Book*, S Fischer-Rizzi, 1988.

thoroughly with the other ingredients and store in an earthenware pot." [24]

In *On Isis and Osiris*, Plutarch says of Kyphi:

"Kyphi is a mixture composed of sixteen ingredients; of honey and wine, raisins and galangal, (pine) resin and myrrh, aspalathos and seseli; moreover, of mastic and bitumen, bulrush and sorrel, together with the two kinds of juniper berries (of which one is called major and the other minor), cardamom and sweet flag. And these ingredients are not mixed by chance, but according to instructions cited in holy books, that are read to the incense makers while they mix them."

About a century after Dioscorides, Claudius Galen (129-201 CE) provided the final variation in his work On Antidotes. Galen lists raisins, wine, honey, asphaltum, bdellium, camel grass [lemon grass], sweet flag, cyperus tuber, saffron, spikenard, aspalathos [bois de rose], cardamom, and cassia.

---

[24] *Incense and Libations*, G.E. Smith, 1921.

16. Perfumes & Cosmetics

As well as incense the Egyptians were very fond of their cosmetics. With regular bathing came regular application of perfumes, deodorants and cosmetics. Deodorants were made by mixing incense or perfumed oils with porridge and putting them in the armpits or between the legs.

Every man and woman, regardless of station, took great care of their appearance. Everyone would own a razor for removing body hair, or use creams. Shampoo, hair-colouring and baldness remedies were used widely, and women wore black eyeliner (kohl) or green eye shadow, made from powdered malachite. Cosmetics such as lip gloss, rouge and nail paints were also used.

Many of the ingredients for incense were used in perfumes, like frankincense, myrrh, galbanum, lotus, lily and sweet flag (calamus). Honey and wine were often used as bases for perfumes. Base oils were the same as many used today, like linseed, sesame, almond, olive, safflower, as well as castor oil, moringa and balanos.

For eye paints, powdered minerals were added to goose fat and sometimes honey. Malachite was used for green, lapis lazuli for blue, and galena for black (kohl). Henna and red ochre were used to produce a red colour for use in lip gloss, nail paints and rouge.

Although there are no recipes for soap, the Egyptians were very fond of their cleansing creams. The recipe for a body scrub used by ladies of the court is given in several of the medical papyri. It is made by mixing equal parts of powdered calcite (lime), salt, honey and red natron, grinding to a paste for bodily application daily. Natron is a purifying preservative still available today that was used widely by the ancient Egyptians in mummification, mouth washes and other cleansing ointments. That it is red indicates the presence of iron tinting the natron and colouring it.

Oil of Lilies

One of the most common Egyptian perfumes was Oil of Lilies, these flowers being one of their favourite scents. This oil was the Chanel of its day! The process of making the oil was complex, but considered well worthwhile.

1.   Mix 210g almond oil, 112g sweet flag and 4g myrrh in 50g red wine. Boil and strain.

2. Bruise and soak 75g cardamom in rain water, and add to the oil. Leave to soak then strain.

3. Take 50 lilies, strip of leaves and place in a broad, shallow vessel. Pour 75g of the oil over them, anoint your hands with honey and stir the pot with your hands. Leave for 24 hours.

4. Strain off the oil, pour into another vessel lined with honey, and sprinkle a little salt on it. Remove any impurities as they gather.

5. Take the remaining herbs, add another 75g of oil and 2g crushed cardamom, stir and strain. Sprinkle with salt and set aside. Repeat to make a third batch.

6. Take another 50 lilies, strip as before, and repeat stages 3-5 with them.

7. Take 7.5g myrrh, 2g crocus and 8g cinnamon, beat and sift and add to water.

8. Pour on the first batch of oil, skim the oil off after mixing, and store in small pots.

9. Repeat stage 7 for the other 2 batches of oil.

17. Food & Wine Offerings

Offerings of food were made on a regular basis to statues of the gods. They were also made to honour the dead. To facilitate accuracy for food offerings and feasting for the modern day heka practitioner, I have listed the various foodstuffs that were eaten by the Egyptians.

In addition to the fruits and vegetables listed, and spices used for cooking, incense and medicine, other types of food were also common. Barley (*it*) and emmer (*bedet*) were the main cereal crops, with wheat being introduced in the Late Period. Bread thus formed the major carbohydrate. Barley was also used to make beer, and offerings of beer and bread were very common. Wine (*irep*) was the other common alcoholic drink used. Honey was widely used for sweetening, and in medicine and for incenses as well.

Cattle were eaten and sacrificed, though meat would have been a less frequent meal among the poor. Milk was also widely consumed. Sheep, goats and pigs were all kept but there is no record of them being used in offerings. Milk, wool and cheese were used from the animals that produced them (i.e. sheep and goats). Poultry was also common, including ducks, geese, pigeons, quails and cranes.

Fish was eaten in large quantities, especially by the poor, but again there is no evidence to show it was used in offerings. Salt was available and used for preservation of food and seasoning.

Wine Offerings

The offering of wine comprised up to five parts, these being an address to the deity, the relationship between the offering and the deity, the names and epithets of the deity, the objective of the offering, and a confirmation of the purity of the offering. There are many examples of this, which contain all or most of the five parts. Below is a good example that can be used for any deity, from the temple at Dendara:

> *"Take to yourself wine,*
> *Which I have offered to your ka.*
> *Ruler, how beautiful is your beauty,*
> *May you drink it; may your heart rejoice;*
> *may anger be removed from your face.*
> *It is pure."* [25]

---

[25] *Wine and Wine Offerings in the Religion of Ancient Egypt*, M. Poo, 1995.

Fruits

Name	Latin Name	Egyptian Name	Used from
Apple	Malus sylvcestris	Depeh(t)	19th Dynasty
Carob	Ceratonia siliqua	Djaret	12th Dynasty
Date	Phoenix dactylifera	Bener	Predynastic
Doum Palm	Hyphaene thebaica	Mama / ququ	Predynastic
Fig	Ficus carica	Dab	2nd Dynasty
Grape	Vitis vinifera	Iarret	3rd Dynasty
Jujube	Zizyphus spina-Christi	Nebes	3rd Dynasty
Olive	Olea europaea	Djedet?	13th Dynasty
Persea	Mimusops schimperi	Shawabu	3rd Dynasty
Plum	Cordia myxa	Unknown	18th Dynasty
Pomegranate	Punica granatum	Inhemen	12th Dynasty
Sycamore Fig	Ficus sycomorus	Nehet	Predynastic
Watermelon	Citrullus vulgaris	Beddu-ka	New Kingdom
Wild Banana	Ensete ventricosum	Unknown	18th Dynasty

Vegetables

Name	Latin Name	Egyptian Name	Used from
Bean	Vicia faba	Iuryt	5th Dynasty
Cabbage	Brassica oleracea	Unknown	19th Dynasty
Celery	Apium graveolens	Matet	Roman period
Chickpea	Cicer arietinum	Heru bik	20th Dynasty
Cos Lettuce	Lactuca sativa	Abu	Old Kingdom
Cress	Lepidum sativum L.	Semet	Unknown
Cucumber	Cucumis sativus	Bendet shespet	New Kingdom
Egyptian Bean	Kyamon aegytion	Neheb	27th Dynasty
Garlic	Allium sativum	Kheten?	New Kingdom
Leek	Allium kurrat	Iaqet	20th Dynasty
Lentil	Ervum lens	Aarshan	Predynastic
Melon	Cucumis melo	Sheshpet	Uncertain
Onion	Allium cepa	Hedju	5th Dynasty
Papyrus	Cyperus papyrus	Mehyt	Predynastic
Pea	Pisum cepa	Tehua	12th Dynasty
Radish	Raphanus sativus	Unknown	12th Dynasty
Sedge	Cyperus esculentus	Gyu	Predynastic
White Lotus	Nymphaea lotus	Seshen	Old Kingdom

Common Herbs & Spices

Name	Latin Name	Egyptian	Used from
Aniseed	Pimpinella anisum	Inset?	Pliny
Cinnamon	Laurus cinnamonum	Ti-shepes	20th Dynasty
Conyza	Erigeron aegypticus	Innek?	Unknown
Coriander	Coriandrum sativum	Shaw	18th Dynasty
Cumin	Cuminum cyminum	Tepnen	18th Dynasty
Dill	Anethum graveolens	Imset	18th Dynasty
Fenugreek	Trigonella foenum-graecum	Hemayt	Unknown
Hemp	Cannabis sativa L.	Semsemet	18th Dynasty
Henna	Lawsonia inermis L.	Hnw	21st Dynasty
Juniper	Juniperus phoenicea L.	Wan	5th Dynasty
Mandrake	Mandragora officinarum L.	Reremet	20th Dynasty ?
Marshmallow	Althaea ficofolia	Unknown	Unknown
Moringa	Moringa pterygosperma	Bek	Unknown
Parsley	Apium petroselinum L.	Unknown	Unknown
Peppermint	Mentha piperita L.	Unknown	21st Dynasty
Safflower	Carmathus tinctorius	Kata	Unknown
Thyme	Thymus acinos	Innek?	Unknown

PART IV

THE CEREMONIES & RITES

18. Purification & Sacred Space

Purity

Purity was absolutely essential to the Egyptian magician. If you were not pure, heka would not work. To this end there was a range of taboos that any practitioner was expected to keep to maintain purity.

Taboos

The taboos included:
- Not eating fish or pork.
- Not eating beans.
- Not eating the flesh of any cult animals.
- Not having sex or masturbating.
- Avoiding animals.
- Avoiding impure people, especially menstruating women and ill people.
- Avoiding substances made from animals, like leather and wool clothing.

A magician or priest would also be expected to bathe frequently, i.e. at least twice a day and twice a night, having a ritual bath in cold water before performing any ceremony. If the magic was performed within a temple the bathing would take place in the sacred lake associated with the temple in its grounds. The mouth would be rinsed with a gargle or water and natron, and a Maat feather was often painted on the tongue with myrrh ink to ensure only words of truth were spoken.

In addition to this all body hair was removed on a regular basis, a practice that might not seem very appealing today. However in a desert climate it is easy to see why such a practice would be performed. Magicians and priests were also expected to be circumcised, although evidence suggests that this was not always the case.

Although the system of taboos followed by the priests might seem harsh, it was not followed all the time. Priests would usually serve one month in four in the temple, during which time all the taboos were followed. For the rest of the time the priest would live in the community and not have to maintain the same strict adherences, and could also perform heka for members of the community, supplementing his income!

Preparing Sacred Space

The sanctuary of the God was usually approached through a hall, entered from an open-air courtyard. This marked the transition from the human realm to that of the divine. In terms of our modern lifestyle and houses, we can still emerge cleansed from the primal waters (bath or shower) and walk through the house (courtyard and hall) to enter the divine sanctuary to perform our rites (temple room).

Before performing ritual, the space would be sprinkled with water and swept with a special broom. This practice still occurs today within Wicca. A layer of clean sand would be spread on the ground, which in modern terms would translate as making sure you have vacuumed or swept the floor! The area would then be censed with incense smoke, which may also have had the added benefit of removing insects. A circle might be marked on the floor with an apotropaic wand.

The following recitations are taken from the twenty-nine episodes on the walls of the chapels at the Temple of King Sethos I at Abydos (c. 1300 BCE), and give some of the words and actions performed in preparing the space. There is no complete set available, but the first and eleventh are relevant for preparing your temple space for Egyptian ritual.

Entering the Temple (Episode 1)

Words spoken to Atum:
> *"I have come before thee, the Great One following me, my purification upon my arms. I have passed by Tefnut, Tefnut having purified me. Assuredly, I am a prophet, the son of a prophet of this temple. I shall not linger, I shall not turn back. I am a prophet. I have come to perform the ritual. Indeed, I have not come to do that which is not to be done."* [26]

Spell for cleansing the Sanctuary (Episode 11)

Words spoken to Atum:
> *"I am Horus; I have come seeking for my two eyes; I shall not allow that it should be far from you, Re-Harakhte. Atum, Lord of the Great Mansion, who resides in the Mansion of Menmaetre,[27] behold me carrying it! May you come in peace! It has driven out all your*

---

[26] *The Mechanics of Ancient Egyptian Magical Practice*, R.K. Ritner, 1993.
[27] Menmaetre was a title of Sethos I, so if using this spell insert your own magical name here.

impurities, for you have assembled it, Atum, father of the gods, who resides in the Mansion of Menmaetre." [28]

When within a sacred space, time did not have any meaning to the Egyptians. Stepping into a sacred space was perceived as returning to the beginning of time, to enable the magician to tap into the energies of creation for performing magic. Again we can see the parallel in modern practices of the magic circle being between the worlds.

After ritual vessels and utensils that had been used would be washed in water from the sacred lake, i.e. specially blessed water, as it was believed to have special purificatory powers.

The Hours

As Re journeyed through the sky in his solar barque, he passed through the hours. Each of the twelve hours of the day had a deity who was present on the barque associated with them. Rites could be performed during these hours for these deities if you wish to time them accordingly

Hour	Deity
1	Maat.
2	Hu.
3	Sia.
4	Asbet (a serpent deity).
5	Igeret.
6	Set.
7	Horus.
8	Khonsu.
9	Isis.
10	Heka.
11	The God entrusted with the tow rope.
12	The God who gives protection in the twilight.

Graveyards

Spells were also sometimes performed in graveyards, to attract the assistance of the dead. It was believed the ghosts of those who had died violent deaths, or died young, were more prone to remain around their burial site. These ghosts were perceived as having a lot of heka, as well as akhu. If they could be persuaded by offerings, or compelled, their assistance could greatly empower a spell or ritual and ensure its success.

---

[28] *The Mechanics of Ancient Egyptian Magical Practice*, R.K. Ritner, 1993.

Whilst this may not appeal to us today, it is a technique that was widely used by the ancient Egyptians, especially for fertility and love spells.

Ritual of the Four Balls

A ritual performed in the temple of Osiris at Abydos was for the protection of his corpse from Set. This translates into a magical protection for your temple and house. Each day four clay balls would be thrown, one in each direction. The balls all had the name of one of the lion-headed goddesses on, each representing an aspect of Re's power, and who would protect the space. The balls were thrown to the south (Wadjet), north (Sekhmet), east (Bastet) and west (Sechemtet).

Repellents

Some substances were considered particularly effective for their protective qualities, and in repelling negative entities. These substances included:

Garlic
In the language of the Ancient Egyptians, the word for garlic sounded like the word for harm, and its shape was considered to resemble teeth. For these reasons it was considered a good protection, and was crushed in beer and the mixture sprinkled over houses and tombs at night to protect from ghosts, scorpions and snakes.

Honey
As honey was sweet to living people, it wasconsidered bitter to the dead. This meant that honey could be used to drive away and protect from the spirits of the dead.

Mother's milk
The milk of a nursing mother with a son was considered very powerful as a protection, as it mirrored the divine relationship of Isis with baby Horus.

Saliva
This was considered a powerful substance as it came into contact with the words spoken by the magician, giving it great power. Spitting was used both in healing, and also as a hostile act, e.g. when cursing or banishing.

Sexual fluids
Because of the taboo against sex and menstruation, sexual fluids were considered a powerful repellent when used in spells. The Egyptians seemed to have a peculiar fear of demon semen – one spell was spoken to prevent demons ejaculating in the person's ear whilst they slept!

Urine

This could be used for both positive and negative magic, and was considered a powerful repellent. Urine was also used as a pregnancy test. If a woman urinated on young plants and they lived she was pregnant, if they died she was not!

19. The Egyptian Calendar

The Egyptian worldview contained two main ways of perceiving time – linear and cyclic. The linear progression was the one that people lived within – from past to present to future. However, within this progression not everyone necessarily experienced time at the same rate. An hour in the presence of Re for a departed soul was said to be equivalent to a whole lifetime for a living person.

In *Egyptian Mythology* the author Geraldine Pinch pointed out that the linear progression of time can be seen as being composed of seven distinct stages. These are chaos, the emergence of the creator, the creation of the world and its inhabitants, the reign of the Sun God, the period of direct rule by other deities, the period of rule by semi-divine kings (history), and the return to chaos. We are still in the sixth stage, before the return to chaos, when only the creator and Maat will remain to create the world anew.

The cyclic progression of time was experienced on a daily basis, as the progression of Re from dawn to dusk, and then through the dark hours of night. Each day was divided into twenty-four hours, twelve for the day beginning at sunrise, and twelve for the night beginning at sunset. Thus the length of the hours varied through the year (until standardisation in the New Kingdom), and this can be seen as the origin of the medieval concept of planetary hours.

The world was seen as being created anew each day. When a pharaoh died the dating system was restarted as well, to show a new cycle had begun.

The ancient Egyptian calendar was full of festivals for their deities. Some days were considered particularly auspicious (good days), and some particularly bad and not for practising magic on (bad days). The last five days of the year were known as the demon days and were considered inappropriate for practising magic on, though feasts and celebrations could be held on them.

The calendar was divided into three seasons, each of four months. The three seasons were *Akhet* (Inundation), *Peret* (Emergence) and *Shemu* (Harvest). The names given to them in the Middle Kingdom were used in the area around Memphis. These names were replaced in the New Kingdom with a more widespread set of names.

The months of Akhet were called *Djehuti* (Thoth), *Paope* (The one of Karnak), *Hathor* and *Koiahk* (Ka upon Ka). The months of Peret were called *Tobe* (The Offering), *Mshir* (The one of the censer), *Paremhotep* (The one of Amen-Hotep) and *Parmoute* (The one of Rennutet). Those of Shemu were called

Pashons (The one of Khonsu), *Paone* (The one of the wadi), *Epep* (unknown) and *Mesore* (Birth or Re).

The ancient Egyptian year started with Sirius rising and the inundation of the Nile. Whilst this was around the summer solstice several thousand years ago, it is now around the beginning of August. As the Egyptian months were 30 days each, with the five Epagomenal days at the end of the year (i.e. 27th – 31st July), these have been set against a modern calendar accordingly.

The dates below have been taken from temple calendars from the Middle Kingdom and New Kingdom. Obviously temples to different deities had different calendars, so this is a guide to give some examples for use in personal practice. As a result you will notice that some festivals fall on bad days, although these are obviously not bad days for the specific festivals. There are other dates you will be able to find if you are a devotee of certain of the gods, especially those like Horus and Hathor.

20. Ancient Festivals

The Season of Akhet (Inundation)

Djehuti - 1st month of Akhet

Day	Modern Month - August	Festivals & Feasts	Auspices
1	1st	New Year feast; Rising of Sothis; Feast of Thoth; Feast of Osiris; Marriage of Isis & Osiris; beginning of 3 day festival of Amun	Very good
2	2nd	Festival of Osiris and the Ennead	Very good
3	3rd		Mostly good
4	4th	Festival of Thoth	Mostly good
5	5th		Very good
6	6th		Mostly bad
7	7th		Very good
8	8th		Mostly good
9	9th	Festivals of Amun and Re	Very good
10	10th	Festival of Tefnut	Very good
11	11th		Very bad
12	12th		Very bad
13	13th		Mostly bad
14	14th		-
15	15th	Offerings to Amun to secure a good flood	Mostly bad
16	16th		Very bad
17	17th		Very bad
18	18th		Very good
19	19th	Festival of Thoth, feast of Nuit and Re	Very good
20	20th	Feast of Drunkenness, possibly a Hathor celebration	Very bad
21	21st		Very good
22	22nd	Great Procession of Osiris	Very bad
23	23rd		Very bad
24	24th		Very good
25	25th	Feast of Lights of Isis	Mostly good
26	26th	Day of battle between Horus & Set	Very bad
27	27th	Day of peace between Horus & Set	Very good
28	28th		Very good
29	29th		Mostly good
30	30th		Very good

Paope - 2nd month of Akhet

Day	Modern Month – September	Festivals & Feasts	Auspices
1	31st August	Festival of welcoming Horus	Very good
2	1st September	Day of making offerings to the Gods	-
3	2nd		Very good
4	3rd		Mostly bad
5	4th		Very bad
6	5th		Very good
7	6th		Very bad
8	7th		Very good
9	8th		Very good
10	9th	Procession of Bastet	Very good
11	10th		Very good
12	11th		Very bad
13	12th	Feast of Satisfying the Hearts of the Ennead	Very good
14	13th	Festival of Khnum	Very good
15	14th		Mostly bad
16	15th	Festival of Neith; feast of the Eye of Horus	-
17	16th		Very good
18	17th	Feast of Khnum	Very bad
19	18th	Feast of Amun	Very good
20	19th		Very bad
21	20th		Mostly bad
22	21st		Very bad
23	22nd		Mostly bad
24	23rd		Very bad
25	24th	Feast of Ptah	Very bad
26	25th		Very bad
27	26th	Feast of lighting the fires of Neith	Very bad
28	27th		Very good
29	28th		Very good
30	29th		Very good

Hathor - 3rd month of Akhet

Day	Modern Month – October	Festivals & Feasts	Auspices
1	30th September	Feast of Sekhmet, feast of Hathor	Very good
2	1st October		-
3	2nd		Very good
4	3rd		Very bad
5	4th		Very bad
6	5th		Very good
7	6th		Very good
8	7th		-
9	8th	Feast of Amun	Very bad
10	9th		Very good
11	10th		Very good
12	11th		-
13	12th		Very bad
14	13th		Very bad
15	14th		Very bad
16	15th		Very good
17	16th		Very bad
18	17th	Festival of Hathor	Very bad
19	18th		Very bad
20	19th		Very bad
21	20th	Feast of Maat	Very good
22	21st	Feast of Heka; feast of Shu	-
23	22nd		Very bad
24	23rd		Very good
25	24th		Very good
26	25th		Very good
27	26th		Very good
28	27th	Festival of Hathor	Very good
29	28th		Very good
30	29th		Very good

Koiahk - 4th month of Akhet

Day	Modern Month - November	Festivals & Feasts	Auspices
1	30th October	Festival of Hathor; feast of Sekhmet	Very good
2	31st		Very good
3	1st November		Very bad
4	2nd	Feast of Sobek	Very good
5	3rd		Very good
6	4th		Very bad
7	5th	Feast of Serket	Very bad
8	6th		Very good
9	7th		Very good
10	8th		Very good
11	9th		Very good
12	10th		Very bad
13	11th		Very good
14	12th		Very good
15	13th	Feast of Re, Sekhmet & Bast	-
16	14th		-
17	15th		Mostly bad
18	16th		Very bad
19	17th		Very bad
20	18th	Festival of purifying the ennead, feast of the Lord of Flight (Horus)	Very bad
21	19th		Mostly bad
22	20th	Festival of "Ploughing the Earth"	Mostly good
23	21st		Mostly good
24	22nd		-
25	23rd		-
26	24th		Good
27	25th	Festival of Neith	Mostly good
28	26th		Very bad
29	27th		Very bad
30	28th	Festival of "Raising the Djed Pillar"	Very good

The Season of Peret (Emergence)

Tobe - 1st month of Peret

Day	Modern Month - December	Festivals & Feasts	Auspices
1	29th November	Feast of Khnum, Heka and Thoth; festival of Bastet	Very good
2	30th		Good
3	1st December		-
4	2nd		Very good
5	3rd		Mostly bad
6	4th		Very good
7	5th		Very bad
8	6th		Very good
9	7th		Very good
10	8th	Feast of clothing Anubis	Very bad
11	9th		Very bad
12	10th		Very bad
13	11th	Festival of Hathor and Sekhmet	Very good
14	12th		Very bad
15	13th		Very good
16	14th		Very good
17	15th		Very bad
18	16th		Very good
19	17th		Very bad
20	18th		Very bad
21	19th		Very good
22	20th		Very good
23	21st	Feast of Neith	Very good
24	22nd		Very good
25	23rd		-
26	24th		Very bad
27	25th		Very good
28	26th		Very good
29	27th	Feast of Bastet	Very good
30	28th	Festival of "Raising the Willow"	Very good

Mshir - 2nd month of Peret

Day	Modern Month - January	Festivals & Feasts	Auspices
1	29th December		Very good
2	30th		Very good
3	31st		Very bad
4	1st January		Very good
5	2nd		Very good
6	3rd	Raising the Djed pillar	Very bad
7	4th		Very good
8	5th		Very good
9	6th		Very good
10	7th		Very bad
11	8th	Feast of Neith	Very good
12	9th		Very good
13	10th		Very bad
14	11th	Feast of Hathor	Mostly good
15	12th		-
16	13th		-
17	14th		Very good
18	15th		Very bad
19	16th		Mostly bad
20	17th		Very bad
21	18th		-
22	19th	Feast of Ptah and Horus	Very good
23	20th		Very good
24	21st		Very bad
25	22nd		Very good
26	23rd		-
27	24th		-
28	25th	Feast of Osiris	Very good
29	26th		Very bad
30	27th	Pacifying of Sekhmet	Very bad

Paremhotep - 3rd month of Peret

Day	Modern Month – February	Festivals & Feasts	Auspices
1	28th January	Feast of Khnum-Re, and of Ptah	Very good
2	29th		Very good
3	30th		-
4	31st		Mostly bad
5	1st February		Very good
6	2nd		Very good
7	3rd		Very bad
8	4th		Very good
9	5th		Very good
10	6th		Very bad
11	7th		Very good
12	8th		Very good
13	9th	Feast of Neith	Very good
14	10th		Very bad
15	11th		Very bad
16	12th		Very bad
17	13th		Very bad
18	14th	Feast of Nuit	Very good
19	15th	Festival of Anubis	-
20	16th		Very bad
21	17th		-
22	18th		Very bad
23	19th	Festival of Horus	Very good
24	20th		Very bad
25	21st		-
26	22nd		Very bad
27	23rd		Very bad
28	24th	Festival of Osiris	Very good
29	25th		Very good
30	26th		-

Parmoute - 4th month of Peret

Day	Modern Month – March	Festivals & Feasts	Auspices
1	27th February	Feast of "chewing onions for Bastet"	Very good
2	28th		Very good
3	1st March	Festival of Horus	Very bad
4	2nd		Very good
5	3rd		-
6	4th		Very bad
7	5th		Very good
8	6th		Very good
9	7th		Very bad
10	8th		-
11	9th		Very bad
12	10th		Very bad
13	11th		Very bad
14	12th		Very bad
15	13th		Very good
16	14th		Very good
17	15th		Very bad
18	16th		Very bad
19	17th		Very good
20	18th		Very bad
21	19th		Very bad
22	20th		Very bad
23	21st		Mostly bad
24	22nd		Very bad
25	23rd		Very bad
26	24th		-
27	25th		Very bad
28	26th		Very good
29	27th		Very good
30	28th		Very good

The Season of Shemu (Harvest)

Pashons - 1st month of Shemu

Day	Modern Month - April	Festivals & Feasts	Auspices
1	29th March	Feast of Tefnut	Very good
2	30th		Very bad
3	31st		Very good
4	1st April		Very bad
5	2nd		Very bad
6	3rd		Very good
7	4th		Very good
8	5th		-
9	6th		Very good
10	7th	Festival of adoration of Anubis	Very bad
11	8th		-
12	9th		Bad
13	10th		-
14	11th		Very bad
15	12th		-
16	13th		Very bad
17	14th		Very good
18	15th	Feast of Neith; great feast of Heka	Very good
19	16th		Very good
20	17th		Very bad
21	18th		Very bad
22	19th	Festival of the two goddesses	Very good
23	20th		Very good
24	21st		-
25	22nd		-
26	23rd		Very good
27	24th		Very bad
28	25th		Very good
29	26th		-
30	27th	Feast of Hathor	Very good

Paone - 2nd month of Shemu

Day	Modern Month - May	Festivals & Feasts	Auspices
1	28th April	Festival of the navigation of Anubis	Very good
2	29th		-
3	30th		Very good
4	1st May		Very bad
5	2nd		Very good
6	3rd		-
7	4th	Feast of Uadjet	Very bad
8	5th	Feast of Neith	Very good
9	6th	Feast of lifting up the sky	Very good
10	7th	Procession of Bastet	Very good
11	8th		Very bad
12	9th		Very good
13	10th		Very good
14	11th		Very good
15	12th		Very bad
16	13th		Very good
17	14th		Very bad
18	15th		Very bad
19	16th		Very bad
20	17th		Very bad
21	18th		Mostly bad
22	19th		Very bad
23	20th		Very good
24	21st		Very good
25	22nd		Very good
26	23rd		Very bad
27	24th		Very bad
28	25th		Very good
29	26th		Very good
30	27th		Very good

Epep - 3rd month of Shemu

Day	Modern Month - June	Festivals & Feasts	Auspices
1	28th May	Feast of Ptah	Very good
2	29th		Very good
3	30th		Very bad
4	31st		Very good
5	1st June		Very bad
6	2nd		Very bad
7	3rd		Very bad
8	4th		Very bad
9	5th		Very good
10	6th		Very bad
11	7th		Very bad
12	8th		Very good
13	9th		Very bad
14	10th		Very bad
15	11th	Offerings to Amun for a good flood	Very good
16	12th		Very bad
17	13th		Very bad
18	14th		Very bad
19	15th		Very bad
20	16th		Very bad
21	17th		Very good
22	18th		Very bad
23	19th		Very bad
24	20th		Very good
25	21st		Mostly good
26	22nd		Very good
27	23rd		Very bad
28	24th		Very bad
29	25th	Feast of entering the sky	Very good
30	26th	Festival for Hathor	Very good

Mesore - 4th month of Shemu

Day	Modern Month - July	Festivals & Feasts	Auspices
1	27th June	Maat unites with all the Gods of the heavens	Very good
2	28th		Very good
3	29th		Very bad
4	30th		Mostly bad
5	1st July		Very good
6	2nd		Very bad
7	3rd		Very bad
8	4th		Very good
9	5th		Very good
10	6th		Very good
11	7th		Very bad
12	8th		Very good
13	9th		Very good
14	10th		Very good
15	11th		Very bad
16	12th		Very good
17	13th		Very good
18	14th		Mostly bad
19	15th		Very good
20	16th		Very bad
21	17th		Very good
22	18th		Very good
23	19th		Very bad
24	20th	Festival of Ptah	Very good
25	21st		Very good
26	22nd		Mostly good
27	23rd		Very bad
28	24th		Very good
29	25th		Very good
30	26th		Very good

The Epagomenal or "Demon" Days

1	27th	Feast of Osiris	Very good
2	28th	Feast of Horus the Elder; and Heka the child	Very good
3	29th	Feast of Set – offerings on the altar	Very bad
4	30th	Feast of Isis, the good feast of the sky and earth	Very good
5	31st	Feast of Nephthys	Very good

21. Rituals

The gods were called on during spells. This is because it was believed that by transferring the personal problem onto a cosmic scale, into the realm of the gods, then the aid of the gods, and the use of heka, could facilitate the solution to the problem.

The Egyptians were very fond of repetition when it came to spells. The usual number of repetitions would be one of the sacred numbers: this would be three, four, seven or nine times, depending on the spell. It is likely that the words were chanted rather than simply being spoken, as this was considered more powerful.

Spells were guarded fiercely, as they were believed to lose their effectiveness if people who were not properly trained in the magical arts spoke them.

As with subsequent magical traditions, spells usually comprised two major aspects – the rubric (spoken words) and the associated actions. Strictly speaking there was generally a third component, which were the ingredients used to help ensure the spell worked.

1) Anti-Demon or Ghost spell
This spell is ideal for those having problems with supernatural activity at their home who want it dealt with permanently. The spell calls on the ferocious cat goddess Mafdet, however it does have the drawback of requiring a cat who embodies the goddess by playing its part in the spell, as will be seen. The magician must bake a phallus shaped loaf, and then wrap it in fatty meat, and feed it to the cat saying the words below. As the cat eats the food physically, the goddess is perceived as destroying the offending entity astrally.

> *"Oh Mafdet! Open your mouth wide against that enemy, [the male dead], the female dead – do not let me see him!"* [29]

2) Anti-nightmare spell
Words to be said by man when he has a nightmare in his own place. The spell was recited, and then breads and fresh herbs soaked in myrrh and beer rubbed on his face. This was thought to dispel the memory and energy of the nightmare. As with many of the spells, the practitioner identifies with Horus.

> *"Come to me, my mother Isis! Look, I see something which is far from me, on my own city!"*

---

[29] *Magic in Ancient Egypt*, G. Pinch, 1994.

"Look, my son Horus, do come out with what you have seen – so that your dumbness finishes, so that your dream apparitions draw back! A fire will leap out against the thing that frightened you. Look, I have come to see you that I may drive out your vexations, that I may annihilate all ailments.

Hail to you, good dream! May night be seen as day! May all bad ailments brought about by Set, the son of Nuit, be driven out. Victorious is Re over his enemies, victorious am I over my enemies!"[30]

3) Grace

This declaration was found in Edfu. In it the dining table is identified with the Creator God Atum, and Pharaoh with his eldest son Shu, who was created from His saliva. Atum was perceived as creating the food; the king would offer them back to Him on the altar, and then consume them (a practice known as reversion of offerings). The person speaking the words is taking the place of Pharaoh. This is an ideal ritual to use for blessing the food and drink for post-ritual feasting. To be spoken before the meal is commenced:

"O Table God, You have spat forth Shu from Your mouth.
O Table God, may He give to You all that He will have dedicated, since He has become a God who is an emanation, alert, worshipful and powerful. May He dedicate to You every good thing which You will give Him, since He has become Heka. May He dedicate to You every good thing, food-offerings in abundance. May He set them before You and may You be content with them, may Your Spirit be content with them and may Your Heart be content with them forever."[31]

4) House protection spell

The words are to be spoken over garlic, ground and pulverised with beer, to sprinkle over the house at night before daybreak. The protection was thought to ensure that no male or female snake, scorpion, reptile, male or female dead will enter the house.

"That one for the garlic, when you enter this house where the Osiris, the god's father and servant of Min, lord of Senwet, the deceased Wennofer, born of Tantamun deceased, is – to close the mouth of any male snake, any female snake, any scorpion, any reptile that bites with its mouth, that stings with its tail. You will kill them. It is the arms of Re, it is the arms of Horus, it is the arms of Thoth, it is the arms of the Great Ennead, it is the arms of the Little Ennead that will kill their enemies through you. You will injure their heads in that

---

[30] *Ancient Egyptian Magical Texts*, J.F. Borghouts, 1978.
[31] *Practical Egyptian Magical Spells*, R.K. Ritner, 1998.

name 'garlic' of you. You will open your mouth against them in that name "mouth-opener" of you. You will devour them in that name "devourer" of you. You will grind their bodies when some snake comes forth at its time in that name "grinder" of you. Oh White Eye of Horus that has come forth from the earth – "that which strikes the subjects for Horus" is its name – may it protect its Horus from the followers of Set!

You will close the mouth of any male snake, any female snake, any scorpion, any reptile. They will not enter this house where the Osiris, the god's father and servant of Min, Lord of Senwet, Wennofer deceased, born of Tantamun, is. The heat of your flame is directed against them: you will kill them, they will die from your grimness." [32]

5) Love Spell

This spell comes from a 20th Dynasty pottery fragment, and illustrates several principles involved in heka. Reference is made to the seven Hathors and the use of red thread, and also includes a threat to Osiris to ensure success.

"Hail to thee, O Re-Harakhte, Father of the Gods!
Hail to you, O ye Seven Hathors
Who are adorned with strings of red thread!
Hail to you, ye Gods lords of heaven and earth!
Come [make] (woman's name) born of (woman's mother's name) come after me,
Like an ox after grass,
Like a servant after her children,
Like a drover after his herd!
If you do not make her come after me,
Then I will set fire to Busiris and burn up Osiris." [33]

6) Migraine Cure

Many magicians seem to suffer from migraine, so this spell is one that is worth trying out if you do. The magician is identifying with Horus the Younger as the migraine sufferer, and ligatures used to bind the pain and move it away from the head. This spell is said over seven threads of a garment, made into seven knots, and placed on the left foot of a man.

""My head, my head," said Horus the Elder.

"The half of my head, the half of my head," said Thoth.

---

[32] *Ancient Egyptian Magical Texts*, J.F. Borghouts, 1978.
[33] *Ancient Egyptian Magic* by Bob Brier, 1980.

"Act for me, mother Isis and aunt Nephthys! Give me your head in exchange for my head, the half of my head!"
"Just as I have seen these people[34] so I have heard these gods[35] saying to me on behalf of my son Horus: 'Let there be brought to me your head in exchange for my head. "

"Let threads be brought from the edge of a garment, having been made into seven knots, placed on the left foot of [name] born of [Mother's name]. What is placed below will cure what is above, for I have elevated what the gods seek."[36]

7) Protecting a Book

There are few people as protective of their book collection as magicians, or as unforgiving when books are stolen. This is a trait that has been with practitioners for thousands of years, as this spell from the *Bremner-Rhind Papyrus* illustrates. It could be spoken over the books of one's book collection as a passive curse, only activated by someone actually stealing it. The person is then bringing the negativity onto themselves, and you cannot be held responsible. Leave it in the hands of Maat!

"As for any man, even of any foreign land, whether of Nubia, Cush, or Syria, who shall remove this book, carrying it off from me - their corpse shall not be buried; they shall not receive cool water; their incense shall not be inhaled; no son or daughter shall wait upon them to pour water offerings to them; their name shall not be remembered anywhere on earth; they shall not see the rays of the solar disk. But, as for any servant who shall see this book, when he has caused that my soul and my name be enduring with praises - there shall be done the like for him after death in exchange for what he has done for me."[37]

8) Protection against Food Poisoning

Copies of this spell were found at Edfu, Esna, and Kom Ombo. They work on the principle that food poisoning occurred as an act of malice. They also imply non-physical poisons, i.e. malice and insidious vindictiveness. This spell could hence be used to send back negativity towards a person causing trouble. As the arrows of Sekhmet are invoked, by the principle of sympathetic magic the malicious individual would then be encouraged to have food poisoning.

"O Sekhmet of yesterday, Wadjet of today,

---

[34] Human sufferers.
[35] Horus the Elder and Thoth.
[36] *Practical Egyptian Magical Spells*, R.K. Ritner, 1998.
[37] *Practical Egyptian Magical Spells*, R.K. Ritner, 1998.

You have come and replenished this table of [name] just as you did for your father Re, when you came forth from the cult city of Pe.
Protect [name] with that papyrus wand of life, which is in your hand, in that name of yours of Wadjet.
Shoot your arrow against all the food of him who shall speak against [name] by means of any evil matters. Let a slaughter be made of them like that time when you overpowered the enemies of Re in the primordial age in that name of yours of Sekhmet.
Your offerings belong to [name]
He is Re from whom you came forth.
So long as he exists, you will exist, and vice versa" [38]

9) Spell for drinking Beer (prophylaxis for Hangover)
This spell is said during the drinking of beer, to be spat up. It was considered very effective, having been proved millions of times! Lady of Hetepet is a title of Hathor as goddess of drunkenness.

"Hail to you Lady of Hetepet! There is no restraining Set when he has set his heart on conquering a heart in that name of his of "Beer," to confuse a heart, to conquer the heart of an enemy, a fiend, a male ghost, a female ghost, etc." [39]

10) Spell against people using the Evil Eye
This spell was used to break bad luck, when it was not known who was wishing bad luck on the person.

"Sekhmet's arrow is in you, the heka of Thoth is in your body, Isis curses you, Nephthys punishes you, the lance of Horus is in your head. They treat you again and again, you who are in the furnace of Horus in Shenwet, the great god who sojourns in the House of Life! He blinds your eyes, oh all you people, all nobles, all common people, all the sun-folk and so on, who will cast an evil eye against Pediamunnebnesuttowi[40] born of Mehtemweskhet[41], in any bad or ominous manner! You will be slain like Apep, you will die and not live for ever." [42]

---

[38] *Practical Egyptian Magical Spells*, R.K. Ritner, 1998.

[39] *Practical Egyptian Magical Spells*, R.K. Ritner, 1998.

[40] The name of the individual in the spell – you would replace this with your own name.

[41] The mother's name of the individual in the spell, likewise replace with your mother's name.

[42] *Ancient Egyptian Magical Texts*, J.F. Borghouts, 1978.

11) Spell for warding off a haemorrhage

This spell was said over a bead of carnelian, which was then applied to the anus of a woman or man to ward off haemorrhage. The spell uses a word play, the word for Hermopolis being *wnw*, and the word for moment being *wnw.t*.

> *"Backwards, you who are on the hand of Horus! Backwards, you who are on the hand of Set! The blood that comes from Hermopolis was warded off; the red blood that comes forth at the moment is warded off! Have you ignored the dam? Backwards you, from Thoth!"* [43]

12) Trampling one's enemies

The Egyptians believed that treading on one's enemies showed your superiority, hence the many depictions of Pharaohs and deities trampling their enemies. This simple spell follows this principle, with the words being spoken as a thin metal sheet with the name of the enemy on is inserted between the foot and the sandal.

> *"My enemy is under the soles of my feet."*

13) Spell for the last day of the year

This is an interesting example of the heka worked in the demon days at the end of the year, when it was thought Sekhmet would punish people who had acted badly. By performing this spell on the last day of the year (the day before the five Epagomenal days) the individual would be protected from her plagues for the coming year. The words were spoken by a man with a club in his hand, who then walks around the house, thus ensuring he will not die of plague during the next year.

> *"Retreat disease demons! No breeze will reach me so that passers-by would pass on, to rage against my face. I am Horus who passes along the wandering demons of Sekhmet. Horus, sprout of Sekhmet! I am the Unique One, the son of Bastet – I will not die on account of you!"* [44]

14) Spell for Protection

This spell draws on the power of the gods of the five Epagomenal days by combining their forms in an amulet. Osiris, Horus, Set, Isis and Nephthys were all drawn onto a clean piece of white linen on the first of the five days, and the following words spoken four times. The linen amulet was then worn around the neck for the five days.

---

[43] *The Magical Texts of Papyrus Leiden*, J.F. Borghouts, 1978.
[44] *Ancient Egyptian Magical Texts*, J.F. Borghouts, 1978.

"Hail to you! O great ones according to their names, children of a goddess [45] who have come forth from the sacred womb, lords by virtue of their father [46], goddesses by virtue of their mother, who do not know the necropolis. Behold, may you protect me and save me. May you make me prosperous and protect me. I am one who is on their list." [47]

---

[45] I.e. Nuit.

[46] I.e. Geb.

[47] *Ancient Egyptian Magical Texts*, J.F. Borghouts, 1978.

22. Thoughts on Practising Heka

If you wish to practice heka and follow the ancient Egyptian methodology there are a number of considerations to take into account, preparations and decisions to make.

Purity

To what level are you going to follow the strictures on purity and taboos? Whilst removing body hair and circumcision may be a bit extreme, adopting the strictures on cleanliness, and the dietary, clothing and sexual taboos is definitely worth considering to a degree that you can manage.

This means removing beans, fish and pork from your diet for a period of time before performing a ritual, or even altogether if you are performing rituals on a regular basis. Consider whether you will be able to do this and still maintain a healthy diet, or can compromise and remove one or two if this is going to cause problems. Likewise check on the symbolic animals associated with the deities you work with, as the flesh of these was also avoided. So for example you would not eat beef if you were working with the cow goddess Hathor.

How do you feel about having to avoid sex for a period of time before performing rituals, or not masturbating? If you are a very sexual person this could again be difficult and you need to consider this carefully. Is a reduction in your sex life acceptable, or will it cause relationship problems for you?

Another taboo that may cause problems is avoiding animals. If you have cats or dogs, or other pets, this is likely to be impossible. You should however try to ensure that the pets do not go into the space you are using as your temple.

Avoiding people who are ill may seem heartless, but the idea behind this is to maintain your own health so your worship of the gods does not suffer. But if your partner, or child, or work colleagues are ill this stricture is not practical in modern life.

If you are a pre-menopausal woman it will be impossible to avoid menstruating women, as you are one. Living in a busy society this stricture is totally unrealistic unless you plan on becoming a hermit.

Avoiding substances made from animals is also a difficult taboo. Your ritual garb can be made from cotton, as the ancient Egyptians did. Strictly speaking you could use synthetic fibres, but this loses some of the essence of the practice. However avoiding things like wool and leather is not going to be realistically feasible, and so again this stricture is best shelved and applied only to your ritual garb.

Regular bathing is essential for practising heka. Whilst four times a day may seem excessive, you can make sure that you always bathe before performing your ceremonies, and are thus clean and pure for your magic. If you are a man you might also like to consider shaving when you bathe, to at least remove facial hair.

Timing

Timing was absolutely critical for the Egyptians. This means rituals may need to be performed at particular times of day, such as sunrise or noon, and on particular days of the year. How will this fit in with your lifestyle, in such areas as your work life and holidays?

Ingredients

Extensive lists of the appropriate materials and ingredients used by the Egyptians have been included in this book. Within these lists there is plenty of scope for using appropriate items without needing to spend huge sums of money or import things.

Being properly prepared also means making sure you have any appropriate spell ingredients, food and drink for offerings, suitable incense, etc, ready before your workings.

Equipment

This is a big issue that needs a lot of consideration. Essential items you will need for your temple space are as follows:

- A small statue of Maat, for the presentation of Maat
- Appropriate statues of deities you wish to work with, or at least good pictures so there are representations for the deity to live in during your rituals.
- White, red, green and blue pieces of cloth for dressing statues.
- A white cotton robe. You can see the designs from the costumes worn by the deities in the images in this book.
- Censer for incense.
- Fan for spreading incense smoke.
- Knife made of flint, obsidian or iron, for "Opening the Mouth" ceremony on your statues.
- Charcoal blocks.
- Appropriate incenses to burn – ingredients and blends are given earlier. Kyphi, frankincense and myrrh are essential.

- Blank papyrus (or paper if you cannot obtain it) for writing on.
- Ink and pen to write with. If you can make your own ink from myrrh resin this is ideal.
- Candles and appropriate candlesticks. You can use white candles always, or beeswax if you wish to. The ancient Egyptians did not use different colour candles in the spectrum of colours now available to us.
- Ointment for anointing your statues with.
- A tray for carrying items on – made of a suitable material, i.e. appropriate wood or metal, but not plastic.

Optional items you may wish to use include:
- A large ankh to carry in your hand.
- A Uraeus crown to wear.
- A sistrum for shaking.
- Appropriate sceptres or wands to wield, particularly if you plan on working with other creatures apart from the gods.

Setting up your Temple

Once you have obtained all the equipment you are planning on using, you need to make sure your temple space is purified and properly set up first. Lighting should be by candles or oil lamps only. The absence of modern technology in the temple as far as possible is also preferable, i.e. no telephones, computers, televisions, etc.

The first thing you should do is walk around the room clockwise, sprinkling water everywhere. Water from a sacred well or spring is ideal for this. You should then sweep the floor with a broom, again moving clockwise, following the course of the sun. Next you should walk around the room censing it with incense.

Mastic as a cleansing scent that is pleasing to the gods would be appropriate, as would frankincense as the pre-eminent Egyptian scent, and it also has purifying properties. Or you might decide you wish to copy the Egyptian marking of Re's journey, and burn frankincense at dawn, myrrh at midday and kyphi at sunset. Symbolically this honouring of Re and marking the daily cycle is highly appropriate for attuning your temple to the energies of heka.

After this you should perform the Spell for cleansing the Sanctuary:

> *"I am Horus; I have come seeking for my two eyes; I shall not allow that it should be far from you, Re-Harakhte. Atum, Lord of the Great Mansion, who resides in the Mansion of (your magical name), behold me carrying it! May you come in peace! It has driven out all your*

> *impurities, for you have assembled it, Atum, father of the gods, who resides in the Mansion of (magical name)."* [48]

Any statues that you are going to use in your temple should have the opening of the mouth performed on them to prepare them for use in your temple. If you cannot find or afford appropriate statues, you can use pictures of the deities as a vessel and gateway for them, and you should perform the opening of the mouth on the image in the same way as you would for a statue.

Movement

As the course of the sun was so vital to the Egyptians, movements in the temple should always be sunwise, i.e. clockwise. To move against the course of the sun (anti-clockwise) would be considered an act of chaos, and against the principles of Maat. Steps should be measured and dignified, and good posture maintained – do not slouch or hurry as this is showing disrespect.

The different movements used, like the invocation posture or recitation of glorifications, should always be employed when performing invocations. Likewise anointing is always done with the little finger of the preferred hand. The more ritualistic and formulaic you make your movements, the better.

Speech

Words being so vital, you should make a big effort to intone words, not just say them. Really focus on putting your intent into the words you intone. Invocations and spells may be repeated four times or even seven times to give them more power and show your devotion.

Visualisation

As has already been mentioned, the Egyptians saw their deities as usually standing about 4.5m (15' or so) high. So if you are meditating and visualising a deity, this is the height you should see it. Remember also to visualise the skin and eyes (if known) the appropriate colour. The deity should be visualised carrying his or her specific symbolic tools. If there are none the deity can always be visualised holding a large ankh as the symbol of life in the right hand.

---

[48] *Ancient Egyptian Magical Texts*, J.F. Borghouts, 1978.

Revising your Practices

Although the ancient Egyptian view inspired much of modern magical practice, you need to put any ideas you have based on your modern experience aside.

The idea of having to cast a circle beforehand for instance, is not an issue in a room that is a consecrated temple space, as the Egyptians would consider that with the deities living there nothing negative is going to try and enter the space. If you are in a place away from your temple, then you could use an apotropaic wand to draw the boundaries of a circle on the floor, as this was an Egyptian practice.

Likewise the convention of the four elements at the quarters does not apply to the Egyptian worldview. If you feel really uncomfortable without the usual forms of protection you invoke, you could invoke the guardian deities associated with the directions in funerary practices as guardians. In this instance you would then invoke Serket in the East, Isis in the South, Neith in the West and Nephthys in the North. This would be done after step 3 in the ritual form given below.

Modern pagans enjoy having cakes and wine at the end of ceremonies, but this is not part of Egyptian practice. When you have left the temple after the rite is finished, you may partake of the offerings, so they are not wasted, as the ancient Egyptian practitioners did.

The opening of circle performed at the end of modern magical ceremonies is not performed, as the temple space is set up as a permanent magical space, and so you simply leave the space in the manner described in step 8 below. If you are away from your temple, you could draw the circle again with the apotropaic wand to open it, but again go clockwise as you visualise your circle disappearing, so you do not act in a chaotic manner.

Ritual form

The following ritual form is a modern reconstruction of techniques and recitations that we know were used by ancient practitioners of heka. It is designed to give a structure to work within, and may be expanded as desired.

Before the ritual you should already have made sure your robe and statue dressing cloths are clean, had a ritual bath, robed and perfumed yourself, and cleaned the temple. Anoint yourself on your brow, heart and arms when you perfume yourself. The brow represents your psychic senses, the heart is your centre of intelligence (in the Egyptian worldview), and the arms to keep within them the words of recitation (i.e. "my purification upon my arms").

1. On entering the room you should begin by reciting appropriate words for entering the temple:

> "I have come before thee, the Great One following me, my purification upon my arms. I have passed by Tefnut, Tefnut having purified me[49]. Assuredly, I am a prophet, the son of a prophet of this temple. I shall not linger, I shall not turn back. I am a prophet. I have come to perform the ritual. Indeed, I have not come to do that which is not to be done."

Additionally you could also use the words spoken to Pharaoh, adapted into the first person:

> "Hu is in my mouth, Sia is in my heart: my speech is the shrine of Maat."

2. Circumambulate the temple clockwise, sprinkling pure water on the floor. You may find it useful to have a tray, with the water on, together with food and wine offerings, censer of incense, fan, Maat statue and dressing cloths, otherwise it can get very complicated if practising by yourself. As you pass the altar you can put the tray down and continue your circumambulation with the water. Then circumambulate the temple a second time with the censer of incense and fan.

3. Recite the ritual "to make protection by magic". You may wish to perform the *Recitation of the Glorifications* sequence of gestures while you say this to give added emphasis to your words.

> "I am that pure Heka who is in the utterance and body of Re. On your face, enemy of Re! I am his ba, the Heka."

---

[49] As Tefnut is moisture and water, this could be seen as a reference to the pre-ritual bathing.

4. Presentation of Maat
Kneel and offer the statue of Maat in the left hand to a statue or image of a deity on your main altar (such as Re or Atum). Your left arm should be bent, but the palm kept horizontal, with the right hand raised in protection of the goddess. Say:

> *"The offering is done for him who has given life*
> *I have brought Maat to you in order that you may live on her*
> *I give you Maat with my left hand, my right hand protecting her."*

5. Dressing of appropriate statues, including offerings
Remove the red cloth left from the previous day for purification. Next purify the statue with water and incense. Now dress the statue in white to safeguard it from its enemies, then after a minute or so remove the white cloth and place blue cloth on it to hide the face. After another minute replace this with green cloth for bodily health, then finally a minute later remove the green cloth and cover the statue with red the for cloth protection. Dab your little finger in ointment and lightly touch it to the statue's forehead.

6. Offerings of wine and food are made to the statue(s) of the deities on your altar. As you place the items on the altar say:
> *"O (Deity Name) Take to yourself wine (or food),*
> *Which I have offered to your ka.*
> *(Deity name), how beautiful is your beauty,*
> *May you drink it; may your heart rejoice; may anger be removed from your face.*
> *It is pure."*

7. Perform your spells or ritual, or any more devotions. Remember that spells were usually repeated four times.

8. Say farewell to any deities you called upon, repeating the farewell so it is said 7 times in total.

9. Perform the Removing the foot - stepping backwards from the altar to the door. You thus leave the shrine in its original state, symbolically returning it to the time of creation. Remove offerings and take them with you when you leave – the deities have had time to absorb the essence from them for their pleasure.

APPENDIXES

A. Sau - Amulets & Talismans

Amulets were a part of everyday life to the ancient Egyptians. Amulets were worn to ward off the misfortunes of fate, especially protection from animal bites and stings, and problems with pregnancy and childbirth. Amulets were also used extensively to protect the dead on their journey through the underworld. Mummies have been found with dozens of amulets wrapped in the wrappings, strategically placed at different parts of the body.

Talismans to attract particular qualities, like permanence and good health, were used to a similar high degree of regularity as the many amulets.

The magic of amulets and talismans was called Sau, and there were dedicated practitioners whose profession was exclusively making these. The two main types of amulet and talisman were those written on papyrus, and those carved in crystal or made of faience.

Those who could afford them wore strings of beads made from different crystals, frequently with several different amulets placed amongst the beads. Amulets depicting specific deities were common, especially those connected with childbirth and protection from evil influences.

Common Amulets & Talismans

Ab or Ieb
The Ab is a stylised human heart. The heart as the place of truth was of great importance to the Egyptians, as it recorded all their deeds in readiness for their judgement in the afterlife. Ptah was said to have conceived the universe in his heart before bringing it to manifestation in the Memphite theology. The Ab was commonly made of carnelian. Ab amulets were placed on mummies to show a person spoke the truth and encourage the granting of entrance to the underworld. Ab's were also included in necklaces like the uset.

Ankh
The ankh sign is the hieroglyph for life, and it was known as the *key of life*. Wearing an ankh was thought to extend the life of the wearer, and deities were frequently depicted carrying an ankh. Belief in the power of the ankh as a talisman to preserve good health and promote longevity survives today.

The Evolution of the Ankh
The ankh is such a popular and universally attractive symbol that it has become used throughout history in many ways. Hence the astrological sign for Venus is derived from the ankh, with the loop rounded into a circle. Early Coptic Christians adopted the ankh, calling it the crux ansata or eyed-cross, as a symbol of the resurrection of Jesus. Today many modern pagans and Wiccans wear the ankh as a symbol of the continuity of the ancient gods.

Anubis
Anubis figures were popular as a protection against evil influences, especially restless ghosts.

Ba
The Ba was depicted as a human-headed falcon with an offering bowl and represents the soul. The combination of the falcon, associated with the sun gods Ra and Horus, with the human head, shows the divine spark present in the soul. By placing the Ba on a mummy it showed the soul was ready to move on. Initially the Ba represented the spiritual manifestation of a deity, but as time went by it became seen as the spiritual manifestation of humans as well, hence the use in funerary rites.

Bastet
Bastet figures were worn to protect from snakes as Bastet killed the Apophisep serpent in one version of the myth. They were also given as gifts on New Year's Day to ward off misfortune in the coming year.

Bes
The ugly dwarf god was very popular and Bes figures were worn to protect pregnant mothers and newborns.

Cartouche
The word cartouche is a modern one, bestowed by the Napoleonic French on the sign, which was known to the ancient Egyptians as shenu, from the verb *sheni* meaning *to encircle*, which is also used for the Shen amulet. The Shenu was used to write names within, as a protective device, and in a modern context obviously lends itself to sigillisation, containing a sigil within it. The Shen depicted as a circle with a horizontal line touching the base. The shen was often depicted in drawings, and rings made in this shape, to draw on its properties as representing eternity and protection. Using a Shen talisman was believed to attract permanence to endeavours.

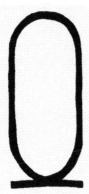
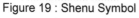

Figure 19 : Shenu Symbol   Figure 20 : Shen Amulet

Cippus
A cippus (plural cippi) was a statue-stela on which Horus was depicted, with spells against venom and bites, for protection from snakes and scorpions. Small ones were sometimes worn or carried and larger ones placed in the house and graves.

Djed pillar

The Djed pillar was a stylised spine and depiction of Osiris, the Djed was sometimes used as shorthand to depict that god and also represent stability and protection. Originally the Djed had been associated with Ptah, who was called the "Noble Djed". The Djed amulet was worn as a sign of stability and regeneration

Figure 21 : Djed Pillar

Horus

Amulets of the hawk god were worn to protect from evil and chaos.

Isis

Isis figures were worn for the protection of Isis, and to encourage strong family bonds.

Menat

The Menat was a wide beaded collar sacred to Hathor, used by women for protection and as a love charm. It symbolised birth, fertility, life, potency and renewal, and was seen as a vessel of transmission of divine power, often depicted being offered to deities, especially Hathor.

Nefer

The Nefer was worn to ensure happiness, youth and good fortune as part of a string of beads. Multiple nefers would imply the idea of beauty and youth. It is a symbolic representation of the heart and trachea.

Ren

A Ren was a person's name written within a Shen, to protect the person. By using an individual's name, it personalised the protection the ren was thought to bring from gods like Horus.

Sa

The Sa was a sign representing protection and magical potency. It is found in amuletic form, and carved on magic wands. The Sa was particularly associated with Bes and Taweret, suggesting it may have been used especially to protect newborns.

Figure 22 : Sa Symbol

Scarab

The classic beetle amulet, representing the god Khephri, was worn to ensure a safe transition from life to death, in the same way that Khephri pushed the sun through the sky like the beetle pushed a ball of dung.

Sekhmet

Sekhmet amulets were given as gifts on New Year's Day to ward off misfortune in the coming year.

Sema
The Egyptians had a good knowledge of anatomy, and were aware of the importance of the lungs, hence the amuletic use of this hieroglyph, which symbolically represented the lungs and the trachea. The Sema was placed on the chest of the mummy to ensure the soul could breathe after death. It was also used as a symbol of union, the trachea and two lungs representing the Nile uniting Upper and Lower Egypt.

Shabti
These small figures were placed in tombs as workers, to perform tasks for the deceased when they were in the underworld so they would not have to. The word *shabti* (or *ushabti*) means *the answerer*, for they answered the call to the soul to perform the actions they were placed there to do. They have obvious potential for use for thought forms for actions like healing.

Taweret
With Bes the hippopotamus goddess was the other popular deity for amuletic protection of pregnant mothers and newborn children.

Tyet
The Tyet, or Girdle or Knot of Isis, was worn around the neck by the living and placed on the neck of the mummy to invoke the protection of Isis. The word *tyet* is often translated as *life* or *welfare*. The Tyet was associated with eternal life and renewal. In later times it was also associated with Hathor, Nephthys and Nuit as well as Isis.

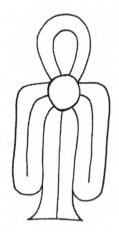

Figure 23 : Tyet / Knot of Isis

Uat
The Uat, or Papyrus sceptre, represented expansion and growth, and the talisman was worn to give energy.

Urs
The Urs or Pillow amulet was placed at the back of the neck of the mummy as a protective headrest. It has also been suggested these amulets were used for lower back problems by the living.

Usekh
The Usekh was a wide beaded collar worn to protect from chest and throat infections. Other charms may be worn in this collar.

The Utchat or Udjat Eye
The Eye of Horus was a powerful protection against evil, and was widely referred to in the medical papyri for use when dealing with eye conditions. Indeed it is still used for both of these qualities.

Figure 24 : Utchat Eye

The Evolution of the Eye of Horus

The Eye of Horus was a very popular design, and has been adopted and used by different cultures throughout history. The Greeks adopted the Eye of Horus, and painted it onto their ships so they could "see" where they were going. The freemasons also adopted the eye of Horus and use it in their symbols as the eye in the triangle.

The eye in the triangle has also found its way onto the Great Seal of the United States and the one dollar bill! And the left-facing eye is also the origin of the pharmacist's symbol for prescription Rx.

B. Dream Interpretation

Dreams were an important part of life to the ancient Egyptians. Dreams conveyed the sleeper into the realms of the gods. Indeed some texts refer to the sleeping dreamer being immersed in the primal waters of Nun, equating the time asleep with the primeval time before creation.

The analysis of dreams was a highly developed art in Egypt. There were books of thousands of dreams and their interpretations held at some of the temples for dream analysis. The most important of these is credited to Hor of Sebennytos.

Listed below are examples of dreams and the interpretations placed upon them:

Capturing female slave	Good	Gaining satisfaction from something.
Climbing on a mast	Good	Being suspended aloft by your god.
Copulating with a pig	Bad	Being deprived of your possessions.
Drinking blood	Good	Putting an end to your enemies.
Drinking own urine	Good	Eating your son's possessions.
Drinking wine	Good	Living in righteousness.
Eating excrement	Good	Eating your possessions in your house.
Killing an ox	Good	The removal of enemies from your presence.
Picking dates	Good	Finding provisions given by your god.
Seeing a large cat	Good	A large harvest is coming.
Seeing face as leopard	Good	Gaining authority over your townfolk.
Uncovering backside	Bad	You will become an orphan.
Writing on a palette	Good	Establishment of your office.

Particular items and stones each had their own interpretation, e.g. pearl meant "Pharaoh will make good fortune for the dreamer", an object made of galena meant "life will be pleasant after great misfortune", and an alabaster object implied sexual infidelity with a married person. If an object was broken in the dream, it meant that hostility was being directed at the dreamer from a source, which could be determined by other details in the dream.

One of the techniques of interpretation was by looking at similar sounding words. So a dream of a harp (*bnt*) could mean that something evil (*bint*) was happening, or a dream of a donkey (*az*) might imply promotion (*saz*).

Some temples were famous as centres of dream incubation. Here a person could spend the night in a special building, possibly aided by the use of visionary incenses. The dreams could then be aimed at communication with the gods or with deceased relatives to gain insight into the future or discover the root of a problem.

The following techniques for dream visions are from British Museum *Papyrus No. 122.*

To obtain a vision from Bes - make a drawing of Besa,[50] on your left hand, and envelope your hand in a strip of black cloth that has been consecrated to Isis and lie down to sleep without speaking a word, even in answer to a question. Wind the remainder of the cloth round your neck. The ink with which you write must be composed of the blood of a cow, the blood of a white dove, fresh frankincense, myrrh, black writing-ink, cinnabar, mulberry juice, rain-water, and the juice of wormwood and vetch.

With this write your petition before the setting sun, [and say],
> *"Send the truthful seer out of the holy shrine, I beseech thee, Lampsuer, Sumarta, Baribas, Dardalam, Iorlex: O Lord send the sacred deity Anuth [51], Anuth, Salbana, Chambré, Breïth, now, now, quickly, quickly. Come in this very night."*

To procure dreams: Take a clean linen bag and write upon it the names given below. Fold it up and make it into a lamp-wick, and set it alight, pouring pure oil over it. The word to be written is this: Armiuth, Lailamchoüch, Arsenophrephren, Phtha, Archentechtha. Then in the evening, when you are going to bed, which you must do without touching food [or, pure from all defilement], do thus. Approach the lamp and repeat seven times the formula given below: then extinguish it and lie down to sleep.

The formula is this:
> *"Sachmu epaëma Ligotereënch: the Aeon, the Thunderer, Thou that hast swallowed the snake and dost exhaust the moon, and dost raise up the orb of the sun in his season, Chthetho is thy name; I require, O lords of the gods, Seth, Chreps, give me the information that I desire."* [52]

---

[50] A form of Bes.
[51] A name of Osiris.
[52] *Egyptian Magic* by E.A. Wallis Budge.

BIBLIOGRAPHY

Bibliography
Allen, James P., Middle Egyptian, Cambridge University Press, Cambridge, 2000
Altenmuller, Hartwig, Apotropaia, Lexikon der Äegyptologie I: 1975
Andrews, C.A.R., Amulets of Ancient Egypt, British Museum Press, London, 1994
-----------, Ancient Egyptian Jewellery, British Museum Press, London, 1990
Assmann, J., Egyptian Solar Religion in the New Kingdom: Re, Amun and the Crisis of Polytheism, London, 1994
-----------, The Search for God in Ancient Egypt, Ithaca, 2001
-----------, Agyptische Hymnen und Gebete, Zurich, 1975
Bagnall, R.S., Egypt in Late Antiquity, Princeton, 1993
Baines, J., Fecundity Figures, Warminster, 1985
-----------, Ankh-sign, belt and penis sheath, Studien zur atlagyptischen Kultur 3 (1975): 1-24
Bakir, Abd El-Mohsen, The Cairo Calendar, General Organisation for Government Printing Offices, Cairo, 1966
Barta, W., Sechem, Lexikon der Äegyptologie V: 772-6
Betz, Hans Dieter, The Greek Magical Papyri in Translation, University of Chicago Press, Chicago, 1996
Blackman, A.M., The King of Egypt's Grace before Meat, Journal of Egyptian Archaeology, vol. 31 (1945): 57-73.
-----------, The Significance of Incense and Libations, Zeitscrift fur Aegyptische Sprache und Altertumskunde 50, (1912): 69-75
---------, Gods, Priests and Men: Studies in the Religion of Pharaonic Egypt, London, 1998
Bleeker, C.J., Hathor and Thoth, Leiden, 1973
Bonner, C., Studies in Magical Amulets Chiefly Graeco-Egyptian, Ann Arbor, Michigan, 1950
Borghouts, J.F., The Magical Texts of Papyrus Leiden I 348, Leiden: 1971.
-----------, Ancient Egyptian Magical Texts, Nisaba volume 9, E.J. Brill, Leiden, 1978
-----------, The Evil Eye of Apophis, Journal of Egyptian Archaeology 59, 1973
Brier, Bob, Ancient Egyptian Magic, Harper Collins Publications, New York, 1980
Brunner, H., Das Herz im Umkreis des Glaubens, Biberach, 1965
Brunner-Traut, Emma, Gesten, Lexikon der Äegyptologie II: 573-85
Bryan, C.P., The Papyrus Ebers, Geoffrey Bles, London, 1930
Budge, E.A. Wallis, Amulets and Talismans, University Books, New York, 1968
-----------, Amulets and Superstitions, Dover, London, 1930
-----------, Egyptian Magic, RKP, London, 1901
-----------, The Mummy, Wings Books, New Jersey, 1989
Buhl, M-L., The Goddesses of the Egyptian Tree Cult, Journal of Near Eastern Studies 6 (1947): 80-97

Cruz-Uribe, E., Atum, Shu, and the Gods During the Armarna Period, Journal of the Society for the Study of Egyptian Antiquities 25 (1995): 3-7

David, Rosalie, Religion and Magic in Ancient Egypt, Penguin Books, London, 2002

Dawson, R., The Number "Seven" in Egyptian Texts, Aegyptus 8 (1927): 97-107

Derchain, P., Le Papyrus Salt 825, Brussels, 1965

Dick, M.B. (ed), Born in Heaven, Made on Earth: The Making of the Cult Image in the Ancient Near East, Winona Lake, Indiana, 1999

Dioscorides, The Greek Herbal of Dioscorides, Oxford, 1934

Dolinska, M., Red and Blue Figures of Amun, Varia Aegypticaa (1990) 6:1-2; 3-7

Doxey, D.M., Anubis, Oxford Encyclopaedia of Ancient Egypt Vol. 1: 97-98

-----------, Sobek, Oxford Encyclopaedia of Ancient Egypt Vol. 3: 300-01

-----------, Thoth, Oxford Encyclopaedia of Ancient Egypt Vol. 3: 398-400

Edwards, I.E.S., Hieratic Papyri in the British Museum. 4th Series. Oracular amuletic decrees of the Late New Kingdom. (2 vols), British Museum Press, London, 1960

El-Sabban, Sherif, Temple Festival Calendars of Ancient Egypt, Redwood Books, Liverpool, 2000

Englund, G., Gifts to the Gods – A Necessity, for the Preservation of Cosmos and Life. Theory and Praxis, in Gifts to the Gods: Proceedings of the Uppsala Symposium 1985, Uppsala, 1987, pp57-66

-----------, Offerings: An Overview, Oxford Encyclopaedia of Ancient Egypt Vol 2, pp564-69

Erman, A., A Handbook of Egyptian Religion, Constable, London, 1907

Fairman, H.W., The Triumph of Horus, London, 1974

Faulkner, R.O., The Bremner-Rhind Papyrus – II, Journal of Egyptian Archaeology, vol. 23 (1937): 11.

-----------, The Bremner-Rhind Papyrus – IV, Journal of Egyptian Archaeology, vol. 24 (1938): 22-24

-----------, The Ancient Egyptian Pyramid Texts (2 volumes), Oxford University Press, Oxford, 1969

-----------, The Ancient Egyptian Coffin Texts (3 volumes), Warminster, 1973

-----------, The Ancient Egyptian Book of the Dead, British Museum Press, London, 1985

Fischer, H.G., The Ancient Egyptian Attitude towards the Monstrous, in Monsters and Demons in the Ancient and Medieval Worlds: 13-26, Mainz, 1987

Fischer-Rizzi, Susanne, The Complete Incense Book, Sterling Publishing Co. Inc, New York, 1988

Foster, John L., Hymns, Prayers and Songs: An Anthology of Ancient Egyptian Lyric Poetry, Scholar's Press, Atlanta, 1995

Gardiner, A.H., Professional Magicians in Ancient Egypt, Proceedings of the Society for Biblical Archaeology 39, 1917

-----------, Egyptian Grammar, Oxford Press, London, 1973

-----------, Hieratic Papyri in the British Museum, 3rd series: 1-11, London, 1935

Gardiner, A.H. & & Sethe, K., Egyptian Letters to the Dead, Egypt Exploration Society, London, 1928

Giveon, R., Skarabäus, Lexikon der Äegyptologie V: 968-81

Goyon, Jean-Claude, Une formule solennele de purification des offrandes dans les temples ptolémaïques, Chronique d'Égypte, vol. 45, no. 90 (1970): 267-81.

Griffith, F.L. & Thompson, Herbert, The Leyden Papyrus: An Egyptian Magical Book, Dover, New York, 1974

Griffiths, J.G., The Origins of Osiris and His Cult, Leiden, 1980

Gunn, Battiscombe, Interpreters of Dreams in Ancient Egypt, Journal of Egyptian Archaeology 4: 252 (1917)

Hansen, N.B., Snakes, Oxford Encyclopaedia of Ancient Egypt Vol. 3: 296-99

Hart, G., A Dictionary of Egyptian Gods and Goddesses, London, 1986

Helck, W., Messer, Lexikon der Äegyptologie IV: 109-13

Hollis, S.T., Five Egyptian Goddesses in the Third Millenium BC, KMT: A Modern Journal of Ancient Egypt 5:4 (1994): 46-51, 82-5

Holmberg, S., The God Ptah, Lund, 1946

Hornung, E., Conceptions of God in Ancient Egypt: The One and the Many, Cornell University Press, New York, 1982

Houser-Wegner, Khonsu, Oxford Encyclopaedia of Ancient Egypt Vol. 2: 233

-----------, Nefertum, Oxford Encyclopaedia of Ancient Egypt Vol. 2: 514-16

-----------, Shu, Oxford Encyclopaedia of Ancient Egypt Vol. 3: 285-86

-----------, Taweret, Oxford Encyclopaedia of Ancient Egypt Vol. 3: 350-51

Iverson, Erik, Some Ancient Egyptian Paints and Pigments, Copenhagen, 1955

Janjuhn, D., Das Buch, Schutz des Hauses, Bonn, 1972

Johnson, J.H., The Demotic Magical Spells of Leiden 1 348, Oudheidkundige Mededelingen het Rijksmuseum van Oudheden te Leiden 56

Kozloff, A.P., Sculpture: Divine Sculpture, Oxford Encyclopaedia of Ancient Egypt Vol. 3: 242-46

Lange, H.O., Der magische Papyrus Harris, Copenhagen, 1927

Legge, F., The Magic Ivories of the Middle Empire, Proceedings of the Society for Biblical Archaeology 27-28, 1905-06

Lesko, B.S., The Great Goddesses of Egypt, University of Oklahoma Press, USA, 1999

-----------, The Ancient Egyptian Book of Two Ways, Berkeley, 1972

Lichtheim, Miriam, Ancient Egyptian Literature (3 volumes), University of California Press, Los Angeles, 1973-1980

Lucas, A. & Harris, J.R., Ancient Egyptian Materials and Industries, Histories & Mysteries of Man, London, 1989

Lurker, M., The Gods and Symbols of Ancient Egypt, Thames & Hudson, London, 1980

Malek, J., The Cat in Ancient Egypt, University of Pennsylvania Press, Pennsylvania, 1997

Manniche, Lise, An Ancient Egyptian Herbal, British Museum Press, London, 1999

-----------, Ancient Luxuries. Fragrance, Aromatherapy and Make-up in Pharaonic Egypt, London, 1999

Martin, G.T., Scarabs, Cylinders and other Ancient Egyptian Seals, Warminster, 1985

Martin, K., Was-Zepter, Lexikon der Äegyptologie VI: 1152-4

McBride, D.R., Nun, Oxford Encyclopaedia of Ancient Egypt Vol. 2: 557-58

Meeks, D., Daily Life of the Egyptian Gods, John Murray, London, 1997

-----------, Genies, anges, demons en Egypte, Genies, Angels, Demons, Sources Orientales 8, Paris, 1971

Meltzer, E.S., Horus, Oxford Encyclopaedia of Ancient Egypt Vol. 3: 123-26

Morenz, S., Egyptian Religion, Ithaca, USA, 1973

Moret, A., Du sacrifice en Egypte, Revue de l'histoire des religions 57 (1908): 57

Müller-Winkler, C., Schen-Ring, Lexikon der Äegyptologie V: 577-9

Mysliwec, K., Atum, Oxford Encyclopaedia of Ancient Egypt Vol. 1: 158-60

Newberry, P.E., Scarabs. An introduction to the study of Egyptian seals and signet-rings, London, 1908

Ogdon, Jorge R., Observations on a Ritual Gesture, After Some Old Kingdom Reliefs, Journal of the Society for the Study of Egyptian Antiquities X.1 (1979): 71-6

-----------, Studies in Ancient Egyptian Magical Thought I. The Hand and the Seal, Discussions in Egyptology I, 1985

-----------, Studies in Ancient Egyptian Magical Thought III. Knots and Ties, Discussions in Egyptology III, 1987

Otto, E., Ancient Egpytian Art: The Cults of Osiris and Amon, New York, 1967

Petrie, Flinders, Amulets, T.N. Foulis Ltd, London, 1914

-----------, The Arts & Crafts of Ancient Egypt, T.N. Foulis Ltd, London, 1909

Piankoff, A. & Clère, J.J., A Letter to the Dead on a Bowl in the Louvre, Journal of Egyptian Archaology 20: 157-69 (1934)

Pinch, Geraldine, Magic in Ancient Egypt, British Museum Press, London, 1994

-----------, Egyptian Mythology, Oxford University Press, Oxford, 2002

-----------, Votive Offerings to Hathor, Griffith Institute, Oxford, 1993

Plutarch, De Iside et Osiride, University of Wales Press, Swansea, 1970

Poo, M., Wine and Wine Offerings in the Religion of Ancient Egypt, Kegan Paul International Ltd, London, 1995

Quirke, S.J.G., The Cult of Ra, Thames & Hudson, London, 2001

-----------, Ancient Egyptian Religion, British Museum Press, London, 1992

Raven, Maarten J., Magical and Symbolic Aspects of certain Materials in Ancient Egypt, Varia Aegypticaa 4.3 (1988): 237-42

-----------, Wax in Egyptian Magic and Symbolism, Oudheidkundige Mededelingen het Rijksmuseum van Oudheden te Leiden 64

-----------, Resin in Egyptian Magic and Symbolism, Oudheidkundige Mededelingen het Rijksmuseum van Oudheden te Leiden 70

Ray, J.D., Cults: Animal Cults, Oxford Encyclopaedia of Ancient Egypt Vol. 1: 345-48

Reymond, E. A. E., From Ancient Egyptian Hermetic Writings (MPER 11), Bruder Hollinek, Vienna, 1977

Ritner, R.K., The Mechanics of Ancient Egyptian Magical Practice, Studies in Oriental Civilization 54, Chicago, 1993

-----------, Practical Egyptian Magic Spells, Presented at the 1998 Oriental Institute Dinner

Roberts, A., Hathor Rising: The Power of the Goddess in Ancient Egypt, Rochester, Vermont, 1997

Romano, J.F., The Origin of the Bes-Image, Bulletin of the Egyptological Seminar 2 (1980): 35-56

Saffiro, L., Food and dietary habits in ancient Egypt, Journal of Human Evolution 1: 297-305

Schafer, Peter & Kippenberg, Hans G., Envisioning Magic, Brill, Leiden, 1997

Shaw, I. & Nicholson, P., British Museum Dictionary of Ancient Egypt, British Museum Press, London, 1995

Shafer, B.E. (ed), Religion in Ancient Egypt: Gods, Myths, And Personal Practices, Routledge, London, 1991

Simon, C., Neith, Oxford Encyclopaedia of Ancient Egypt Vol. 2: 516

Smith, G.E., Incense and Libations, Bulletin of the John Rylands Library 4 (1921): 191-262

Sourdive, C., La Main dans l'Egypte Pharaonique, Berne, 1984

Spiegelberg, W., Demotische Papyrus aus den koniglichen Museen zu Berlin, Giesecke & Devrient, Leipzig, 1902

Staehelin, E., Menit, Lexikon der Äegyptologie IV: 52-3

Teeter, Emily, The Presentation of Maat: Ritual and Legitimacy in Ancient Egypt, Chicago, 1997

-----------, Maat, Oxford Encyclopaedia of Ancient Egypt Vol. 2: 319-21

Te Velde, H., Seth, God of Confusion, Leiden, 1967

-----------, The God Heka in Egyptian Theology, Jaarbericht van het Voorasiatisch-Egyptisch Genootschap "Ex Oriente Lux" 21, 1970

Tobin, V.A., Theological Principles of Egyptian Religion, New York, 1989

Traunecker, C., The Gods of Egypt, Ithaca, 2001

Ucko, P.J., Anthropomorphic Figurines of Predynastic Egypt and Neolithic Crete, London, 1968

Vandier, J., Le Papyrus Jumilhac, Paris, 1961

Venus, Pascal, The Gods of Ancient Egypt, Tauris Park Books, London, 1998

Vischak, D., Hathor, Oxford Encyclopaedia of Ancient Egypt Vol. 2: 82-85

Von Kanel, F., Scorpions, Oxford Encyclopaedia of Ancient Egypt Vol. 3: 186-87

Watterson, B., The Gods of Ancient Egypt, Gloucestershire, 1996

Wells, R.A., The Mythology of Nut and the Birth of Ra, Studien zur atlagyptischen Kultur 19 (1992): 83-91

Wildung, D., Egyptian Saints: Deification in Pharaonic Egypt, New York, 1977

Wilkinson, Alix, Ancient Egyptian Jewellery, Methuen & Co. Ltd, London, 1971

Wilkinson, Richard H., Symbol & Magic in Egyptian Art, Thames & Hudson, London, 1994

----------, The Complete Gods and Goddesses of Ancient Egypt, Thames & Hudson, London, 2003

Wilson, H., Egyptian Food and Drink, Shire Publications, Princes Risborough, 1988

Witt, R.E., Isis in the Ancient World, Baltimore, 1997

Zakbar, L.V., The Theocracy of Armarna and the Doctrine of the Ba, Journal of Near Eastern Studies 13 (1954): 87-110

Ziegler, C., Sistrum, Lexikon der Äegyptologie V: 959-63

INDEX

Index

T

U

V

W

About the Author

David Rankine is a writer and researcher living in London, UK and is well known for his workshops and lectures on a variety of esoteric subjects.

He has been involved in a number of Western Mystery Traditions since the 1970's. In addition to his deep rooted passion for the Egyptian Tradition, he has also studied Qabalah, Renaissance & Medieval European and Celtic traditions of magic.

In addition to this book, David is also the author of a number of other books, which include *"Circle of Fire"* & *"The Guises of the Morrigan"* (both co-authored with Sorita D'Este); *"Climbing the Tree of Life"* and *"Becoming Magick"*. He is also co-producing the *Sourceworks of Ceremonial Magic* series, which include *"The Practical Angel Magic of Dr John Dee's Enochian Tables"* and *"Keys to the Gateway of Magic"* with well-known occult author Stephen Skinner.

In addition to spending his time researching and writing books, David is also a regular contributor to a variety of esoteric and MBS magazines and journals. He also leads regular workshops and gives lectures around the UK and Europe on subjects related to ancient spirituality, magic and ritual.

When he is not writing or researching, he can usually be found reading, listening to music or catching up with correspondence.

If you would like to find out more about his work, or have comments on this book that you would like to share, please visit his website at www.ritualmagick.co.uk or write to:

David Rankine
c/o BM Avalonia
London
WC1N 3XX
England